D0985999

The Economy of Salvation

The Economy of Salvation

Essays in Honor of M. Douglas Meeks

EDITED BY

Jürgen Moltmann,
Timothy R. Eberhart, *and* Matthew W. Charlton

CASCADE *Books* • Eugene, Oregon

THE ECONOMY OF SALVATION
Essays in Honor of M. Douglas Meeks

Copyright © 2015 Wipf and Stock Publishers. All rights reserved. Except for brief quotations in critical publications or reviews, no part of this book may be reproduced in any manner without prior written permission from the publisher. Write: Permissions, Wipf and Stock Publishers, 199 W. 8th Ave., Suite 3, Eugene, OR 97401.

Cascade Books
An Imprint of Wipf and Stock Publishers
199 W. 8th Ave., Suite 3
Eugene, OR 97401

www.wipfandstock.com

ISBN 13: 978-1-62032-628-2

Cataloging-in-Publication data:

The economy of salvation : essays in honor of M. Douglas Meeks / edited by Jürgen Moltmann, Timothy R. Eberhart, and Matthew W. Charlton ; foreword by Matthew W. Charlton ; preface by Jürgen Moltmann.

xii + 166 p. ; 23 cm. —Includes bibliographical references.

ISBN 13: 978-1-62032-628-2

1. Meeks, M. Douglas. 2. Economics—Religious aspects—Christianity. 3. God. I. Moltmann, Jürgen. II. Eberhart, Timothy R. III. Charlton, Matthew W. IV. Title.

BR115.E3 E27 2015

Manufactured in the U.S.A.

New Revised Standard Version Bible, copyright 1989, Division of Christian Education of the National Council of the Churches of Christ in the United States of America. Used by permission. All rights reserved.

Contents

Foreword

This volume of essays is presented to M. Douglas Meeks in honor of the significant gifts he has offered to the church and the academy. As editors, we are grateful, first and foremost, to Doug Meeks: for the personal and professional relationships we share with him, for his kindness and generosity to his students, and for his deep love for the church. We are also grateful to the contributors to this volume who, through the gift of their time and talent, seek to honor Doug by offering a contribution to the ongoing theological dialogue with his work.

The process of bringing this volume to completion has spanned at least seven years, beginning with a discussion among some of Doug's students at the Twelfth Oxford Institute of Methodist Theological Studies, held at Christ Church, Oxford. It should be noted that, for many years, Doug has been the organizing force behind the Oxford Institute, which is a significant gathering for the worldwide Wesleyan communion. As time went on, we would work on bits and pieces of the project, but it really began in earnest in the spring of 2012. Shortly after an invitation went out to contributors, we began receiving affirmative and enthusiastic responses, sometimes with a chapter attached. Cascade Books, an imprint of Wipf and Stock, responded swiftly and affirmatively with an offer to publish this book.

Early on, we were grateful to have the involvement of Jürgen Moltmann, who agreed to serve as the General Editor as well as contribute a foreword and chapter to the volume. Tim Eberhart has been absolutely fundamental to this project and has taken on the lion's share of the work with the contributors to bring it to fruition, in addition to writing the commendable introduction to this volume. To all who had a part in this volume, I express my deepest gratitude.

Over the years of my association with Doug Meeks, first as teacher, then doctoral examiner and friend, he has consistently emphasized two themes that must predominate in the vocation of the clergy. First, those who seek to serve the church as pastors must be theologians. Their first and most important task is to communicate for the church and the world the grace of God incarnate in Jesus Christ. When pastors lose sight of this, they become administrators of a dying nonprofit. When pastors grasp hold of the centrality of speaking of God, they become prophets in a world deeply in need of, but likely not desiring, the disorienting word. This leads to the second theme: we need prophetic leadership in the church. He once described this to me by saying that the church needs more "rascals" in leadership: people who are called to speak the Word of God and willing to embody that Word in their own lives. Accordingly, rascal-theologian pastors speak the truth, with a heart full of love and grace for God's hurting world, to the pain of the whole world. They speak God's *oikonomia* of freedom and salvation to economies that bind and enslave. This is tough work, because very few people actually like rascals or theologians who speak their minds as they seek to embody God's grace. Doug's legacy is represented far beyond the contributors to this volume. His legacy is represented by a long line of rascal-theologian pastors, denominational leaders, bishops, professors, and laypeople who have found their vocational purpose through Doug's labors.

There are several people who helped in large and small ways with bringing this book of essays to completion. First, we wish to thank two splendid copy editors, Blair Meeks and Eleanor Moore, both of whom carefully read through the text and helped create a manuscript that was consistent and beautiful. Second, special thanks to Blair Meeks and Angela Flanagan for translating chapters from German and Spanish, respectively. Third, a word of personal thanks to Michael Nausner for delivering the first version of the manuscript to Professor Moltmann's front door in Tübingen, saving a good amount of postage. Finally, everyone who has worked on this book, from the editors to the contributors, has done so out of gratitude for the life and work of M. Douglas Meeks. To God be the glory.

Matthew W. Charlton

Preface

"In Praise of Friendship"

"A friend is someone who likes you." Thus begins a wonderful children's poem by Joan Walsh Anglund. And so began the friendship, more than fifty years ago, between Elisabeth and me and Doug and Blair Meeks. Such deep and true friendship, with warm affection and respect, is gained from binding one's own freedom with others. Out of pleasure in our friendship, I seize the opportunity in this foreword to thank Doug and Blair for their love.

Our friendship began as Elisabeth and I came with our four children to a guest professorship at Duke University in 1967. My unforgettable colleague Fred Herzog asked Doug Meeks to become my student assistant. Doug assisted me not only academically but also by introducing us to American life in the Southern states. He attempted to explain American football two times, but as the Blue Devils lost two times, he was doctoring a headache. We learned to treasure American jazz when the Preservation Hall Jazz Band came to Duke; we heard the protest singer Pete Seeger; and we celebrated American Christmas. At the end of our time, we drove to Blair's parents near Clifton Forge in the blooming Virginia spring. One year later Doug and Blair were with us in Tübingen, and in 1971 Doug took his doctorate with a well-received dissertation, *Origins of the Theology of Hope* (Fortress, 1975). When I came to lecture in the United States, I visited him, whether he was at Huntingdon College in Montgomery, Alabama, or at Eden Theological Seminary, St. Louis, or at Wesley Theological Seminary in Washington, or at Vanderbilt University, Nashville. Alternately, they came to see us in Tübingen or when Elisabeth and I were in America. I baptized their first son, Douglas, with Neckar River water in the Church of St. Martin in Tübingen and their second son, John, with Mississippi River water in the Eden Seminary Chapel. Doug translated several of my books, including

The Passion for Life (Fortress, 1978), which he also edited. I remember well the day of January 24, 1978. At Candler School of Theology's 43rd annual Minister's Week, in the large church at the gate of Emory University, Doug presented me with the one hundredth copy of this English edition, and I presented him with the 101st. The exchange was grand. In the book there is also a chapter on "Open Friendship," the experiential background for which I thank Doug and Blair. Peter Slade has made a whole book of this topic: *Open Friendship in a Closed Society: Mission Mississippi and a Theology of Friendship* (Oxford University Press, 2009). Thus the experiences and ideas multiplied and spread.

In 1989, Doug published his significant book *God the Economist: The Doctrine of God and Political Economy*, with Fortress Press. It soon saw a second edition and was translated into other languages. In my early years, Johann Baptist Metz and I had developed a "political theology," a Christian theology "with its face to the world." The world has changed fundamentally since that time: the political is governed by the economic, which has itself globalized, while the political has remained particular. We need an economic and ecological theology if we are to account for our Christian hope with its face to the world. Doug Meeks helps us to this end. His 1989 book that joined theology and economy gave us, so to speak, an appetizer. We eagerly await the new dish of the main course, his masterwork on theology and economy, on which he has worked for years. When he finally—as we say in Germany—"emeritizes," and with that is free from academic responsibilities, a great and beautiful task waits for him. We wish him the delight of the Holy Spirit in this work. This Festschrift should make him bold.

Jürgen Moltmann
Tübingen

Contributors

Walter Brueggemann is Professor Emeritus, Columbia Theological Seminary, Decatur, Georgia.

J. Patout Burns is Professor Emeritus of Historical Theology, Vanderbilt Divinity School, Nashville, Tennessee.

John B. Cobb Jr. is Professor Emeritus of Theology, Claremont School of Theology, Claremont, California.

Timothy R. Eberhart is Assistant Professor of Theology and Ecology at Garrett-Evangelical Theological Seminary in Evanston, Illinois, and the Methodist Theological School in Ohio, in Delaware, Ohio.

Néstor O. Míguez is Professor of New Testament, ISEDET University Institute, Buenos Aires, Argentina.

Jürgen Moltmann is Professor Emeritus of Systematic Theology at Universität Tübingen, Tübingen, Germany.

R. Kendall Soulen is Professor of Systematic Theology, Wesley Theological Seminary, Washington, DC.

Marjorie Hewitt Suchocki is Professor Emeritus of Theology, Claremont School of Theology, Claremont, California.

Michael Welker is Professor of Systematic Theology and Director of the Internationales Wissenschaftsfourm at the University of Heidelberg, Heidelberg, Germany.

Sondra Wheeler is Martha Ashby Carr Professor of Christian Ethics, Wesley Theological Seminary, Washington, DC.

Charles M. Wood is the Lehman Professor Emeritus of Christian Doctrine at Perkins School of Theology, Southern Methodist University, Dallas, Texas.

Josiah U. Young III is Professor of Systematic Theology, Wesley Theological Seminary, Washington, DC.

1

Introduction

TIMOTHY R. EBERHART

For the last four decades, M. Douglas Meeks's wide-ranging contributions to theological reflection and education, pastoral formation, and public witness have placed him at the center of many of the most important developments in contemporary North American theology. Those who know Doug's scholarship are undoubtedly familiar with his groundbreaking work in exploring and articulating the radical political-economic implications of the core affirmation that the triune God—the divine Economist who is Father/Mother, Son, and Holy Spirit—is at work in and for the salvation of the world by "making home" for the whole creation. Countless church leaders, from World Council of Churches representatives to bishops, clergy, and laity, have received his gifts of clear guidance, faithful instruction, and poetic inspiration. Those who have sat in Doug's classroom and around his seminar table know that he is an exacting but gracious teacher who expects his students to think as deeply as he does about the nature of God and God's righteousness, the mission of the church, and the unjust sufferings of the poor. Most everyone who knows him has experienced the warm hospitality Doug and his wife, Blair—a wise theologian herself, and a skilled liturgist— freely offer within their home and throughout their lives, both of which are far along the *via salutis* toward Christian perfection in *this* life.

This book of essays is offered with great respect and appreciation in honor of M. Douglas Meeks, who is a colleague, teacher, scholar, administrator, mentor, friend, minister of the Gospel, advocate for the poor, and disciple of Jesus Christ through the Holy Spirit. It contains essays that address the theme of God's economy of salvation from biblical, historical, ecclesial, and theological perspectives. We hope this volume serves both to recognize and celebrate this influential and beloved theologian and to focus attention upon the *oikonomia* of God's righteousness, which Doug continually reminds us is the saving power of God for life over death. In his introductory lectures to beginning theology students, Doug often claims that Christian theology can only be done in conversation with others. The contributors to this collection, most of them longtime friends, colleagues, and collaborators, are a tribute to the depth and breadth of Doug's living conversation partners. All have written out of sincere respect and grateful affection for M. Douglas Meeks.

The focal theological themes present within Meeks's corpus are many: hope in God's coming reign of righteousness within the whole of creation; the suffering love of God manifest on the cross; the *perichoresis* (round dance) of God's triune life together; the sanctifying grace of the Holy Spirit empowering us to participate in Jesus' resurrection life already here and now under the conditions of history; God's particular concern for those threatened by death—the poor, oppressed, homeless, abandoned, vulnerable; and a vision of political economy for both the church (given in the Eucharist) and the nations (achieved through political struggle and reform) that corresponds more closely to the inclusive, self-giving, coequal, communal, and just nature of God's economy. Although a full introduction to Meeks's work is not possible here, a brief review of the defining marks of his unique approach to the theological task will, I hope, help frame these rich and varied themes.

A Political Theologian

Following his two primary mentors, Jürgen Moltmann and Frederick Herzog, Meeks has taken up the tasks of political theology by investigating not only the *political* implications of various theological claims but also the *theological* assumptions embedded within any particular political ideology or system. As he often impresses upon his students, it is not enough simply to speak of "God" in church or in public, for we must always ask, "Of which God are you speaking?" The God of Jesus Christ and the Holy Spirit is decidedly *not* the deity of Egypt, Rome, Babylon, or the god called upon by politicians to "bless the United States of America."

At the same time, the absence of explicit God-talk within certain public, secular spheres does not mean God-concepts are not in fact operative in both subtle and powerful ways. One of Meeks's most enduring contributions, in fact, has been to unmask the deformed and oppressive theological conceptions implicit within the modern global market economy. In many of his writings, including especially his masterful and still urgently relevant *God the Economist: The Doctrine of God and Political Economy*, Meeks has shown how traditional Western attributes of God as infinite, immutable, immortal, impassible, omniscient, and omnipotent are fundamentally constitutive of the ideal *homo economicus* underlying the logic of modern political economy. Capitalism's self-interested rational actor who maximizes his utility through market exchange is ultimately a description of the West's Monad of Being who transcends suffering and need in absolute isolation from all others.[1] Meeks has taught us that those seeking more just, equitable, and sustainable systems of property/ownership, work, and consumption—systems that do not terrorize the poor and ravage the biosphere—must engage in criticism of the market economy's implicit theological assumptions while also proposing alternative theological visions that can support the emergence of a very different kind of political economy.

A Church Theologian

The church, according to Meeks, is eligible to contribute toward a critical and constructive public theology for the sake of a more just political economy to the extent that we who are the church's stewards draw deeply and intentionally upon our own biblical, theological, and ecclesial knowledge and memory. Here Meeks shows his allegiance to Karl Barth, with whom both Moltmann and Herzog began their theological careers. To do political theology effectively, then, requires attending to *dogmatics*, which Meeks describes as "the church's way of making a judgment about the truth in the face of the truth claims in the church and the world that contradict Jesus Christ."[2] From Meeks's perspective, the North American church has been silent on matters of economy precisely because it has been so completely absorbed by the theo-logic of the global market. One of the key tasks of the theologian in our context, therefore, is first and foremost to convert our churches to the theo-logic of God the Father/Mother, Son, and Holy Spirit.

1. Meeks, *God the Economist,* esp. ch. 3.
2. Meeks, "Economy and the Future of Liberation Theology," 44.

Only then might we Christians be able to contribute to the shaping of an alternative economy in the world.[3]

In searching deeply within the biblical narratives to uncover the logic of God's Trinitarian history with the world, Meeks identifies a wealth of wisdom internal to the church but available to be shared in public conversation with others about political economy. In recounting the story of Exodus, Meeks shows how crushing debt and the centralization of power and wealth inevitably leads to slavery, while reminding us that God's salvation begins among oppressed peoples as the power for liberation from bondage. He sees the Torah as God's gift to Israel in order to instruct the nations how to order economic life to avoid slavery and serve the flourishing of life through such laws as prohibiting usury, sharing common goods through gleanings and tithing, showing hospitality to foreigners, observing Sabbath rest for workers and the land, and observing the Jubilee redistribution of concentrated wealth. In Jesus' table practices, Meeks says, God's economy is revealed as one in which everyone is invited, especially the poor and those considered strangers, debts are forgiven, dignity is bestowed, gifts are distributed through the logic of grace, power is justly shared, and the resultant abundance is enjoyed by all.[4] A church marked by the active remembrance of this *oikonomia tou theou* would have much to offer the world, indeed.

Because he is a church theologian, Meeks knows that theology is not complete with God-talk alone but entails guiding others to participate in God-walk as well. Here Meeks follows his spiritual elder, John Wesley, in understanding that the teaching role of the theologian includes creating opportunities for practical formation in the ways that lead to life. "Theology as life in the Holy Spirit" by following Jesus Christ, he has written, "is an ordering of one's way of being in the world out of the energies of God's grace."[5] Meeks's lifelong commitment to reform the shape of theological education—guided by Wesley's questions for the early Methodists: What to teach? How to teach? What to do?—has involved participation with students in Covenant Discipleship groups, feeding ministries with the poor, community gardens, prison ministries, public protests against the death penalty, and more. Engaging faithfully in theological education today requires "a constant practical and theoretical struggle before God for a life that conforms to the character of God's life"—a struggle that, Meeks has

3. Meeks, "God's *Oikonomia* and the New World Economy."
4. Meeks, *God the Economist*, ch. 4.
5. Meeks, "Reflections and Open Tasks," 133.

argued, will include attempts to resource the church in its mission to the world, to form direct relationships with the poor and oppressed, and to re-shape seminary life itself in greater conformity to the triune God's economy of salvation.[6]

A Metaphorical Theologian

Perhaps the orienting genius of Meeks's work resides in his poetic language and metaphorical images gifted to the church and world. Precisely as one committed to the formation of persons in ecclesial communities for the sake of a more just and hospitable world, Meeks has disciplined his writing and public speaking so that his penetrating and complex analyses of politi-cal economy, Trinitarian theology, contemporary culture, and ecclesial life are accessible to educated clergy and laity, as well as academics in other disciplines devoted to the common good. Unlike other metaphorical theo-logians of his generation, Meeks has drawn deeply upon the living symbols of the Bible and church that infuse his work with a richness and power that will likely endure long after other, more experimental and well-known attempts have faded from relevancy.

For Meeks, God is the Economist, the homemaker who redeems the world by creating the conditions of home for all God's creatures. *Oiko-nomia* in its ancient usage (*oikos* = household + *nomos* = laws or rules) simply means the management of the household. The most basic question of economy, then, is this: Will everyone in the household get everything they need to live? Home is 1) where everybody knows your name/story, 2) where you can count on being confronted, forgiven, loved, and hoped for, 3) where you can always count on there being a place for you at the table, and 4) where you can trust that what is on the table will be shared with you.

If home is having access to these means of life, according to Meeks, then to be homeless in any of these ways is to be subject to death. He has identified at least six dimensions of the menacing threat of poverty, from which God the Economist provides salvation. For those who cry out "I am hungry" (economic poverty), the scriptures respond that "God is bread." For those who cry, "I have no power to determine my future" (political poverty), Christians affirm that "God is power." For those who cry, "I have no story, no name" (cultural poverty), the church proclaims that "God knows you by name." For those who cry out, "I am ignorant, I don't know"

6. Meeks, "Globalization and the *Oikoumene*," 10.

(educational poverty), the scriptures say that "God is wisdom." For those who cry, "I am sick, I have no health" (bodily/natural poverty), Christians claim that "God is healing." And for those who cry out in despair, "I have no hope" (spiritual poverty), the answer is that "God is hope."

The church, for Meeks, is God's attempt to build a household that will join God in making the world into home. Essential to the flourishing of any home are the material/symbolic elements of table, bread, water, oil, towel, and basin. The church's sacraments, then, are the means by which God creates the conditions of home for the homeless. Having received the gift of home, Christians are thus sent into the world to help make home for all others.[7]

These rich and generative metaphors, along with many others, capture both the substance and methodological approach of Meeks the political church theologian. These will last as one of his most enduring legacies.

Essays

The diverse essays in this volume reflect Meeks's broad influence upon contemporary theological reflection and education, as well as his impact upon the life of the church and the world. Walter Brueggemann offers a reading of the Elijah, Micaiah, and Elisha narratives hidden within 1 and 2 Kings, demonstrating how each provides a prophetic challenge "from below" to the more official accounts of established power and royal claims to authority. Patout Burns's essay provides a comprehensive examination of Augustine's views on wealth, property, earthly goods, social status, poverty, and almsgiving found throughout his sermons. John Cobb reflects on decisions made by the 2012 General Conference of the United Methodist Church concerning homosexuality and proposes a progressive vision for the future of the United Methodist Church rooted in Wesley and oriented around principles of inclusiveness, justice, peace, and sustainability. Kendall Soulen argues that pluralist calls to depict God as the nameless, ineffable One manifest through all religions reflect the logic of the marketplace, proposing instead that the LORD made known to Israel through the exodus and revealed as Jesus Christ is a God who resists commodification and imperial control. Néstor Míguez uncovers the systemic violence woven into the global market economy and its effects upon the peoples of Latin America,

7. The content of this section is drawn from notes taken in Meeks's lectures from multiple courses at Vanderbilt Divinity School over the span of many years.

contrasting neoliberalism's culture of violence with the biblical vision of a culture of peace. Marjorie Hewitt Suchocki argues that Meeks is implicitly a process theologian, pointing to his rejection of Greek philosophical categories of divine omnipotence and omniscience and his affirmation of a God whose power is present in the world to create inclusive communities for the well-being of all. Michael Welker proposes a way forward for christological reflection in the West by demonstrating how a return to teaching the threefold office of Christ—kingly, prophetic, priestly—allows us to focus on the public Christ in different domains of life. Sondra Wheeler reviews Wesley's writings on the use of possessions, identifying the strategies Wesley employed in addressing the structural and material lives of the early Methodists, while suggesting points of contemporary relevance of a Wesleyan perspective on wealth, possessions, and economics. Charles Wood argues that one of the contributions the Wesleyan tradition offers to ecumenical ecclesiological conversations today is viewing the church in the context of the work and presence of the Holy Spirit. Young sets forth a spirituality of hope grounded in the biblical witness and conversant with Meeks's writings, and Moltmann offers up elements of a culture of life and a confidence in the future amidst the many crises threatening existence today.

Conclusion

M. Douglas Meeks began his theological career in a turbulent age marked by political revolution, cultural upheaval, and the cries of the world's poor for liberation and justice. In his first book, revised from his dissertation, *Origins of the Theology of Hope*, Meeks wrote that Christian existence is defined neither by optimism nor pessimism but resides within "the dialectic between hope and our suffering from real contradictions of our humanity."[8] The age today is marked by multiple overlapping crises that threaten the world's poor and the planet's impoverished natural systems with death. The questions that Meeks has attended to for decades are still at the urgent center of theological reflection and education. In an age of climate change and resource depletion, what ought we to hope for in light of the *novum* given to us in the life, death, resurrection, and coming reign of Jesus Christ? Amidst the growing disparity between the wealthy elite and the dehumanized poor caused by a global corporatocracy and justified by a deformed market ideology, how might our political and economic systems

8. Meeks, *Origins of the Theology of Hope*, 7.

be re-shaped such that all enjoy the goods of dignified work, just access to "daily bread," an equal voice in the shaping of society, spiritual and bodily health, and creative participation in communities both local and global? For those of us who work and teach in seminaries and divinity schools—which are experiencing a critical shaking of the foundations as well—what are we to teach, how are we to teach, and what are we to do in the face of a North American church that seems wholly unprepared to address the massive social, political, economic, and ecological crises threatening to overwhelm us? In all of these questions, and many more, Meeks continues to be a wise and faithful guide, directing our hope toward the God who made a people out of no people, who raised the Son from the grave through the Spirit of Life, and who will make this increasingly uninhabitable world into our true and lasting Home.

May this volume honor Doug's significant and ongoing contributions to theology, the church, and the world God so loves, while bearing witness to God's *oikonomia* of salvation.

Bibliography

Meeks, M. Douglas. "Economy and the Future of Liberation Theology in North America." In *Liberating the Future: God, Mammon and Theology*, edited by Joerg Rieger, 43–59. Minneapolis: Fortress, 1998.

———. "Globalization and the *Oikoumene* in Theological Education." In *Ecumenical and Interreligious Perspectives: Globalization in Theological Education*, edited by Russell E. Richey, 3–16. Nashville: QR, 1992.

———. *God the Economist: The Doctrine of God and Political Economy*. Minneapolis: Fortress, 1989.

———. "God's *Oikonomia* and the New World Economy." In *Christian Social Ethics in a Global Era*, edited by Max L. Stackhouse et al., 111–26. Nashville: Abingdon, 1995.

———. *Origins of the Theology of Hope*. Philadelphia: Fortress, 1974.

———. "Reflections and Open Tasks." In *What Should Methodists Teach? Wesleyan Tradition and Modern Diversity*, edited by M. Douglas Meeks, 131–40. Nashville: Abingdon, 1990.

2

A Royal Miracle and Its *Nachleben*

WALTER BRUEGGEMANN

Good years of collegiality and team-teaching have left me greatly indebted to Doug Meeks.[1] The only way I can think to acknowledge that debt is to offer a reading of a text that I hope and intend to be congruent with an interpretive perspective that I have learned from him.

I

The books of 1 and 2 Kings consist of forty-seven chapters that trace the Davidic monarchy in Jerusalem from the death of David to the fall of Jerusalem circa 962–587 BCE, plus a paragraph possibly added some years later (2 Kgs 25:27–30). That long royal recital is largely formulaic, including a verdict of the "good king" or "bad king," a theological judgment commonly attributed to the Deuteronomist. Alongside that recital the text traces the unstable royal dynasties of northern Israel from the schism of 922 to the fall of the northern capital of Samaria in 722 at the hands of the Assyrians. The substance of the books is a roster of established power, "the urban elite" who lived off the produce and wealth generated by peasant agriculture, extracted from them by the well-organized tax system (e.g., 1 Kgs 4:7–19). The formulaic report pauses only occasionally for narrative episodes,

1. My debts to Blair Meeks are comparably great. In a formal introduction for a lecture by Elisabeth Moltmann-Wendel, Blair puckishly added, "Her husband Jürgen is a fine theologian in his own right." So also in Blair's presence, her husband, Doug, is a fine theologian in his own right.

notably concerning Solomon (1 Kgs 3–11), Joash (2 Kgs 11), Hezekiah (2 Kgs 18–20), and Josiah (2 Kgs 22-23). The plot line proceeds on the assumption that the recital of kings constitutes the normative account of the history of Israel and Judah, an assumption that has been largely shared in modern interpretation. The equation of "office holders" and "history" is of course a common assumption among us, given in our memorization of "the kings and queens of England" or the U.S. presidents, a memory that is often supplemented by the list of wars that have been won by the office holders.

The most remarkable literary datum of this forty-seven-chapter chronicle is that it is abruptly and dramatically interrupted by a very different narrative, namely, the accounts of the prophetic appearances of Elijah, Micaiah, and Elisha. The initial intrusion upon the "roster of power" is the appearance of Elijah in 1 Kgs 17:1: "Now Elijah, the Tishbite, of Tishbe in Gilead said to Ahab, 'As the Lord the God of Israel lives, before whom I stand, there shall be neither dew nor rain these years, except by my word.'"

Elijah receives no introduction from the narrator. He is given no pedigree and no social location, except "the Tishbite," a term that helps us not at all. Elijah receives four chapters of reportage (1 Kgs 17–19, 21). He is followed in 1 Kgs 22 (one chapter only) by Micaiah, who is identified only as a "son of Imlah" and is, in the narrative, regarded by the royal office holders as an exception, thought by the king of northern Israel to be often a bearer of bad news to the kings and therefore more likely to offer some reliable word—which he does not in this instance! After him comes Elisha, son of Shaphat, introduced in 1 Kgs 19:19–21, who waits until 2 Kgs 2, at the ascension of Elijah, to begin his extended narrative performance. From that beginning point, he is privileged to have eight chapters of narrative (2–9), plus a belated appearance in chapter 13. The sum of the narratives concerning these prophets, Elijah, Micaiah, and Elisha, amounts to thirteen chapters, not counting the odd narrative of Elisha in 2 Kgs 13. Thus these three inexplicable characters occupy thirteen of the forty-seven chapters of the royal recital, a sizable proportion of the whole.

One readily senses a remarkable disjunction in the attention given to the three. These chapters are quite unlike the formulaic royal recitals. In critical judgment they bear few marks of the Deuteronomic editing.[2] They differ radically from the royal chronicle in content and therefore in theological perspective. Those differences, moreover, are matched by a different

---

2. Noth, *The Deuteronomistic History*, had seen that the prophetic narratives bear few marks of the Deuteronomic historian.

literary articulation. The roster of establishment power is something like a chronicle with the tone and expression of a memo. By contrast these three receive such narrative presentation that scholarship readily labels their reports as "legends," a term that would not be used for royal formulae.[3] While the term "legend" is a form critical usage following Herman Gunkel, there can hardly be any doubt that such scholarly usage also means to suggest that the narratives are fanciful, propelled by playful imagination, and lacking in historical reliability. The contrast of styles is complete between royal report, which has a sense of the "factual" about it, and the prophetic narratives, which proceed in something like playful fantasy that is surely not factually reliable.

Thus we have at the center of the books of Kings an alternative articulation that is at best irreverent toward royal power and that perhaps in its very presentation intends to be subversive of and dissenting from royal claims to authority. Consequently the books might better be titled "Kings?" with a doubting question mark. This "hidden transcript" suggests an alternative account of history, one to which the power roster barely had access,[4] which features different plot lines, different characters, and different outcomes. This account remains "hidden" only because in the ancient draft it is contained within the royal recital and because our modern critical reading scholarship, with its tenured epistemology, has been free to disregard, dismiss, and explain away a version of history "from below" that "from above" seems hardly credible. Thus the books of Kings are put together as a staging ground for a vigorous contestation about the nature of history. Like every such contestation, this one is concerned with the truth of power.[5]

In considering the Elisha narrative, one is struck by the way in which royal figures are treated, if they are treated at all. They are reported in a way that contradicts the "royal recital," so that royal claims to authority are by narrative process largely deconstructed. The narrator takes his time with these interruptions and subversions of royal power. While royal memos can be summarized and routinized, subversive narratives cannot be hurried. They must be relished and lingered over, careful detail by careful detail:

3. Most recently Walzer, *In God's Shadow*, 80, refers to these prophets as "legendary heroes."

4. The allusion is to Scott, *Domination and the Arts of Resistance*. The royal and prophetic scripts compete in the books of Kings, but the prophetic script is "under the radar."

5. See my book *Truth Speaks to Power*.

- In 2 Kgs 4, this subversive character, Elisha, is alone with an economically bereft widow (vv. 1–7). He turns on the widow's spigot of olive oil, saves her house from foreclosure, and recovers her children about to be sold into slavery.

- In the same chapter 4, Elisha receives the defaulted body of the boy, breathes new life into him, and says, without further elaboration, "Take your son" (v. 36).

- In chapter 5, Elisha disregards the status and prestige of the general-cum-leprosy and sends him to the Jordan for recovery (v. 10). Then he sends him home to Damascus to worship his idols with only the blessing, "shalom" (v. 19).

- In chapter 6, Elisha turns out to be a player in the centuries-old Israeli-Syrian war. He prays the enemy into blindness (v. 18); then he prays the enemy back to sight after they have been captured (v. 20). He counters the old and deep hostility with a huge feast; he feeds the enemy (v. 23)! The anonymous, irrelevant king (minus the formulae of royal dignity) wants to kill the Syrians, but he is dismissed, along with his thirst for vengeance, by Elisha.

- Later in chapter 6, Elisha presides over an intense famine. The crisis is that, as in every famine, there is food; but in its shortage, food is too expensive for poor people to buy. The famine is ended because YHWH creates panic among the Syrians, who abandon their food supply. Yet again Elisha anticipates such food that the king is helpless to deliver.

In all these narratives, the prophet, the interrupter of royal power, occupies center stage. He comes without status, intrudes into the royal narrative without pedigree, and enacts transformations "from below."

In this long narrative pause in the royal chronicle, the claims of royal authority are superseded. More than that, they are portrayed as foolish and without force. The king is absent amid the wonders of chapter 4. But then the king appears:

- In the healing of Naaman, the king disclaims any ability to heal: "Am I God, to give death or life, that this man sends word to me to cure a man of leprosy? Just look and see how he is trying to pick a quarrel with me" (5:7).

- In the war with Syria, the king enters the story late, with a thirst for vengeance but without authority: "Father, shall I kill them?" (6:21). He is refuted by the prophet: "No! Did you capture with your sword and your bow those whom you want to kill?" (6:22).

- In the midst of the famine, the king denies the capacity to provide food: "No! Let the LORD help you. How can I help you? From the threshing floor or from the wine press?" (6:27).

That is all! Kings are not life-givers! They are portrayed as inept and impotent. For good reason the king remains unnamed in the narrative, having done nothing to merit identity or reputation.

After this series of episodes of inexplicable pastoral transformation, we come to a political coup instigated by the prophet. In chapter 9, Elisha manages a secret anointing to set in motion a revolution that will place Jehu, the zealot, on the throne in Samaria:

> When you arrive, look for Jehu, son of Jehoshaphat, son of Nimshi; go in and get him to leave his companions, and take him into an inner chamber. Then take the flask of oil, pour it on his head, and say, "Thus says the LORD: I anoint you king over Israel. Then open the door and flee; do not linger" (9:2–3).

The young man dispatched by the prophet does the anointing:

> Thus says the LORD the God of Israel: I anoint you king over the people of the LORD, over Israel; you shall strike down the house of your master Ahab, so that I may avenge on Jezebel the blood of my servants the prophets, and the blood of all the servants of the Lord (9:6–7).

Finally, after resisting disclosure of the treasonable act, Jehu acknowledges the act to his companions: "This is just what he said to me: Thus says the LORD, I anoint you king over Israel" (9:12).

Three times the verb "anoint" is sounded, a sacramental gesture by the prophet that gives legitimacy to a social revolution. In this narrative, Elisha has moved from the pastoral to the political, directly challenging for the first time the legitimacy of the rule of Ahab and his family. Perhaps he judges that pastoral acts are no longer enough to effect change. The action initiated by Elisha in chapter 9 is played out in violence; the death of Jezebel fulfills the anticipation of Elijah (9:3–37; see 1 Kgs 21:23). In chapter 10, a bloody elimination of the entire royal house is performed: "So Jehu killed all who were left of the house of Ahab in Jezreel, all its leaders, close friends, and priests, until he left no survivors" (10:11).

Then comes the death, the violent death, of all those loyal to Baal and the covenant-violating social system legitimated by Baal (10:18–31). This is not a pretty picture that emerges from such determined religious absolutism! The narrator, however, seems to have no other way to imagine regime change except by violence that is grounded in prophetic zeal. Once the prophet disrupts royal continuity, there is no telling!

II

Thus the Elisha narrative consists in two quite distinct arenas. In chapters 4–7, we have a series of intimate pastoral transformations. In chapters 8–10, we witness public actions of violent overthrows of power. Our interest in what follows is the peculiar narrative of 2 Kgs 8:1–6 that seems to mark a divider between these two narrative foci. Two points are important as we move into this narrative. On the one hand, we have in chapters 4–7 a series of texts that discount the unnamed king as inept, impotent, and irrelevant. On the other hand, in chapters 8–10 we have actions initiated by Elisha that have destabilized the northern dynasty of Ahab and furthered rabid religious passion.

It is then a surprise to find the narrative of 2 Kgs 8:1–6 wedged between chapters 4–7 that discounts the king and chapters 8–10 that destabilizes kingship. We are surprised because in this narrative the king is the defining and decisive character. Though still unnamed, the king in this narrative is not inept, impotent, or irrelevant. Rather, this king is fully in charge and is able to act effectively, quite in contrast to the previous articulations of the king.

This narrative opens with two recognizable themes. First, the presenting problem is a famine. While the scarcity of food has been resolved in the narrative of chapters 6–7, the problem is a continuing or recurring one. Food shortages make the cost of food too expensive except for those who are privileged and powerful. The famine, moreover, is to last seven years, perhaps an echo of the old Pharonic nightmare about famine (Gen 41:1–7). The crisis to come upon Israel will be acute in a way that requires emergency action.

Second, the first character presented in the narrative is recognizable: the woman "whose son he had restored to life" in chapter 4. From that earlier text we know that she had a husband (v. 25) and was wealthy (v. 8). She was, moreover, deeply devoted to Elisha, first because she had shown him hospitality (v. 10–11) and second because he had restored her son to life (v. 35–36).

Now in chapter 8, this same woman is in a very different circumstance. First, there is no mention of her husband; perhaps she is a widow, which would make her more vulnerable. We are not told. Second, her previously reported wealth will not protect her in the face of the famine. She is a person in potentially dire circumstance. In the previous story she had been "bitter" about the death of her son (4:27). Now she is advised by Elisha to flee from the famine. She does not ask Elisha to cope with the famine, nor does he offer such help. He is realistic and pragmatic: Go where there is food! She goes away—to the Philistines—for seven years! We are left to conclude, without any data, that she received adequate food during that interim period.

The crisis upon which the narrative turns does not concern where she was among the Philistines, or even the famine. It is rather back home from which she had been absent for seven years. The narrative is terse about her return home. It assumes, but does not report, that she has lost her property. We are not told how this loss occurs, whether in the rough-and-tumble of economics during her absence or in the reassignment of her property by the king. In any case, this once wealthy woman is now without resources. We already know from chapter 4 that she is a woman capable of public business. Here she goes to court. She lodges an "appeal" (8:3). The term "cry" here means to make a formal court complaint. That term, even in such usage, is not without emotive power.[6] The cry—as we know both in narrative (Exod 2:23) and in commandment (Exod 22:23, 27)—is a vigorous assertion that is designed to mobilize social and perhaps even theological power to right a wrong, to correct an injustice.[7] While Elisha had counseled her at the beginning of the seven years, he is not present at her return. Her own initiative has led her to the royal court.

Then the narrative is interrupted. The narrator takes us inside the chamber of the king, who is still unnamed. The king is in conversation with Gehazi, Elisha's rather unsavory aide. We know him from two previous narratives. In chapter 4, he was involved with the crisis of the dead son. First, he tries to push the mother away from Elisha, perhaps to protect his master

6. For a full exposition of "the cry," see Boyce, *The Cry to God.*
7. On such mobilization of social power, see Sheppard, "'Enemies," 61–82.

(4:22). Then he himself addresses the dead child, but to no effect (4:31). His second appearance is at the end of the Naaman episode in which he appears as an extortionist. As payback for his action, he is struck with leprosy (5:19–27). In both narratives, he clearly is not in sync with Elisha's self-presentation. Now in our present episode, he is chatting with the king. We are not told how he gained access to the king. His presence there may make one suspicious: his access to the royal presence might suggest a betrayal of Elisha. The narrative does not comment. The only one who speaks in this exchange is the king, who invites Gehazi to tell about Elisha's "great deeds." This is a most remarkable invitation, because it makes evident that the king knows about Elisha's actions and is curious about them. Of course we do not know if the king's query is ironic or straightforward. If straightforward, the king is impressed by what he has heard of Elisha. If ironic, the king may, not unlike the cynical general in 5:11–12, belittle the performance of Elisha and imagine that in truth this character without credentials could not possibly do "great things."

Either way, the king uses the term "great things," a term not used anywhere else in the Elisha narrative. The royal use of the term would seem to be an acknowledgement that Elisha has indeed performed acts that are beyond royal capacity or explanation. The term is otherwise used in the biblical text for "divine wonders," most particularly the exodus deliverance:

> Just remember what the LORD your God did to Pharaoh and to all Egypt, the great trials that your eyes saw, the signs and wonders, the mighty hand and the outstretched arm by which the LORD your God brought you out. (Deut 7:18–19)

> He is your praise; he is your God, who has done for you these great and awesome things that your own eyes have seen. Your ancestors went down to Egypt seventy persons; and now the LORD your God has made you as numerous as the stars in heaven. (Deut 10:21–22; 29:3; Josh 24:17)[8]

Now the king takes that term from the exodus tradition to refer to Elisha's narrative performance that is, each time, an act that brings new life out of deathly circumstances of leprosy, famine, and war.

Gehazi responds to the king's query, though we do not get a direct quote from him. He focuses in his response, we are told, precisely on the restoration of "a dead person to life," the episode in which Gehazi had been

---

8. The only other usage in Ezek 16:61 is not relevant to our theme.

involved.[9] Gehazi, in his response, is interrupted. Verse 5 is a curious verse. The very character who is the subject of Gehazi's narrative now appears in person. Gehazi stops his narrative and functions as a receptionist, perhaps accepting his role as an aide and not a peer to the king. His announcement of the woman may be for him a verification of his narrative rendition, as though to say to the king, "See, I told you!" Gehazi serves only to bring the woman into the king's presence; he then disappears from the account.

Now the woman is in a new posture. She is not primarily the woman with a dead son; now she is the woman with lost property. She has "appealed" to the king. Thus her script from verse 3 is restated before the king. She is the demanding suppliant in the royal court. She seeks restoration of her property from the king, as she had sought the redress of her son from Elisha. Her script is an insistence that she has been dealt an injustice and that only the king can give restitution. The king interviews the woman in order to get the facts of her case. Having the facts in hand, the king acts quickly and decisively. He designates a court official to oversee the case. The king never verbalizes a verdict, but his actions clearly indicate the royal judgment that an injustice has been perpetrated against the woman and must be corrected. The outcome is the royal verb "restore," with reference to her house and property. The king provides, moreover, that she receive all past revenues from her land during her seven-year absence.

This brief narrative is remarkably complex, made so especially by the character of Gehazi. Yet the plot line of action is not complex. It is restoration in response to the appeal. The appeal is so effective and compelling that the king immediately authorizes restoration. This royal act of restoration, however, is no obvious or sure thing. Indeed, in context it is quite remarkable and unexpected. Kings—leaders of the "urban elite"—are not habituated in granting petitions from lowly losers. More than that, we would not expect such a verdict from an heir of Ahab on two counts. First, as chapters 9–10 indicate, the Ahab dynasty consists in practitioners of Baalism, a practice that is not only religious but that has socioeconomic implications that are imperious to justice claims. Second, we would not expect it because the king's act is a dramatic contradiction of Ahab's (and Jezebel's) action concerning Naboth's vineyard that runs roughshod over old claims of property as heritage.[10] In this case, the king acts against such confiscatory policies that enjoy religious legitimacy.

9. The linkage between historical deliverance and resurrection is given lyrical expression by Paul in Rom 4:17.

10. It occurs to me that this restoration of land is an exact counterpoint to the "take possession" of Ahab and Jezebel in 1 Kgs 21.

We may thus puzzle about how this "great thing" might have happened. I dare to suggest that the king's awareness of Elisha's work and his "great things" provides in the text an unacknowledged impetus and motivation for the king. It is credible to think that the king could recognize that Elisha's restorative performance constituted a challenge to a dynasty that did not do restoration. The king is challenged enough by the prophetic witness that he must move out of his socioeconomic narcoticism to establish himself as capable of restorative acts. The consequence is a "great thing" enacted by the king, a "royal miracle" that comes in the wake of the prophetic miracles. I entertain the thought that there was a kind of "contagion" in the Elisha witness to social possibility that summoned the king to act out beyond conventions of the dynasty.[11] Neither Gehazi nor the narrator comments, and the king is quite terse. The outcome is an answered appeal in which the vulnerable woman receives back what is rightly hers.

III

The Elijah-Elisha narratives linger in the imagination of Israel. They linger as a paradigm for the disruption of worldly power by the elusive power of God that is characteristically enacted by human agents "from below." Such a way of articulating subversive power serves the Gospel narrative in the Christian tradition with regard to John the Baptist and then with regard to Jesus. As Tom Brodie has shown, there cannot be any doubt that the Elijah-Elisha narratives have an important afterlife in the imagination of the Gospel writers.[12] To be sure, this pertains principally to Elijah and much less to Elisha. Indeed, the reference to 2 Kgs 5 and the healing of Naaman in Luke 4:27 is the only explicit reference to Elisha in the New Testament. It should not surprise us, however, to have fewer direct allusions to the Elisha narrative in the church's imagination.

In what follows I consider the probability that the parable by Jesus in Luke 18:1–8 is an important evidence of the afterlife of this narrative from 2 Kgs 8:1–6. The parable is situated in Jesus' instruction to his disciples about

---

11. A compelling example of such "contagion" is the case of F. W. de Klerk in South Africa, who finally engaged the "great things" of Nelson Mandela, perhaps helped along by the witness of Desmond Tutu and the various church leaders who clustered around the Kairos Document.

12. Brodie, *The Crucial Bridge*.

prayer that concerns not "losing heart" (v. 1). After the parable of verses 2–5, the interpretive reflection of verses 6–8 concerns:

- the verdict of the unjust judge;

- a rhetorical question concerning God's grant of justice—a question that requires "yes" as an answer;

- the agency of the ones who cry out in their chosenness;

- the answer in verse 8 to the rhetorical question of verse 7 concerning God's justice.

The text teems with "justice," the cry for justice, and the gift of justice. The final question turns the question of justice to a question of faith. Faith is confidence in God's readiness to do justice. That confidence to pray or to cry out for justice is a refusal to "lose heart." Thus prayer is not merely an act of petition; it is rather an elemental confidence that God does indeed do justice in response to a prayerful cry.

The parable features a widow who petitions for justice so long that she wearies the judge.[13] A desperate widow in need of justice who files an appeal sounds much like a replay of the woman in 2 Kgs 8. There she is not identified as a widow; but she has, in the story, no mentioned husband. She pushes her way into the court of the king with her petition. In the parable the counterpart to the woman is a judge "who neither fears God nor had respect for persons." The unnamed king in 2 Kgs 8 is not characterized in this negative way; but the description of "unjust" might have fit Ahab, his father, and might, in anticipation, be used to describe Ahab's son as well. We have no hint ahead of time that the unnamed king is not unjust like his father and like that belated unjust judge. No reason is given in the older text to expect the king as a final judge to grant justice to the woman. In the same way, there is no reason to expect that the cynical judge in the parable would grant justice to the woman. In both cases, the cry from below impinges upon the authority figure in unexpected ways. In the parable, the judge relents of his cynicism because of the relentlessness of the petitioning widow.

In the older text, we are not told why the king rules in her favor. The only factor that is of interest in the narrative is testimony to Elisha and his "great things" that restore life in a community of desperate need. In the older text, the unnamed king commits a "royal miracle"—"royal" in that it is the work of the king, "miracle" because it is completely counterintuitive

13. Note the alternative translation as given in NRSV: "so that she may not finally come and slap me in the face."

that the king would grant restoration to the woman. It is impossible, in my judgment, to imagine this "royal miracle" except in the context of the prophetic miracles of restoration to which Gehazi witnesses.

In the appeal, the ruling of the judge is no less a "miracle." It is against all odds and violates all the protocols of conventional power and conventional justice. Thus Jesus is summoning his disciples to be bold and counterintuitively confident that the world that appears closed because of indifferent power is potentially open to restorative miracles, made open by the incessant prayer from below that is relentless and without doubt. The miracle of the king, like the later miracle of the judge in the parable, is not "supernatural." It is conducted by a human agent, in this case the judge and in the earlier case by the king. My judgment is that the parable is richer in depth and intensity when it is recognized as a re-performance of the older narrative in which the voice of the one who cries out holds the upper hand over settled power that possesses the gift of justice.

IV

In the sequence that I have pursued—*a*) the Elisha narratives, *b*) the narrative of 2 Kgs 8:1–6, and *c*) the parable of Jesus—we have nothing less than a transfiguration of politics that is inevitably at the same time a transfiguration of religion.[14] In both the texts in 2 Kings and Luke, the formidable representative of establishment power is clear. In Kings, it is the sequence of Davidic rulers, even though our narrative concerns the impressive dynasty of Omri in the North. In the Gospel narrative, the power structure is fully identified in the tradition of Luke:

> In the fifteen year of the reign of Emperor Tiberius, when Pontius Pilate was governor of Judea, and Herod was ruler of Galilee, and his brother Philip ruler of the region of Ituraea and Trachonitus, and Lysanias ruler of Abilene, during the high priesthood of Annas and Caiaphas. (Luke 3:1–2)

The narrative of royal/imperial power is each time disrupted. Just as it is disrupted by Elijah and Elisha in the books of Kings, so it is disrupted in the Gospel narrative by John the Baptizer and by Jesus. In the parable, the

---

14. The phrase is from Lehmann, *The Transfiguration of Politics*. Lehmann's argument continues to be pertinent among us.

disciples are summoned to be continuing disruptors of settled power that is self-serving and biased against justice for those below:

- The narratives of Elijah and Elisha attest that the royal narrative is capable of interruption. Again and again, the Elisha narrative attests to the dysfunction and therefore the irrelevance of royal power. In 2 Kgs 8, it is as though for an instant, under the tutelage of Elisha, this heir of Ahab comes to awareness and acts against royal protocol for the sake of the petitioning woman in front of him. He does a "great thing"!

- The parable of Jesus, an echo of that older narrative, exhibits the way in which judicial power, surely authorized by king or by empire, can be interrupted for the sake of justice. The unjust judge does a "great thing"! Even the rulers of the empire (of the "Medes and Persians") are vulnerable to the cry from below when it is loud and long enough (see Dan 6:8, 15)![15]

- Yet the parable is a parable, a parabolic witness to the way of God. "Prayer" may be addressed to a king who belongs to the family of Ahab or to a judge authorized by Rome. But at the end, prayer is addressed to God who, in response to the cry, will "quickly grant justice."

Thus all systems of power are penetrable in heaven and on earth. None of them is settled, closed, and fixed. It is only those "above" who imagine that all is settled, closed, and fixed and who, by ideological practice, recruit those "below" into that despairing conviction. In the end, however, those from "below" know better. This is the "hidden transcript" that refuses to accept the public transcript from above.[16]

In our context, the slogan of "class warfare" recurs in political life. It is ironic (or predictable!) that that accusatory phrase is most often on the lips of those "above" who accuse those below of "advocating class warfare." By that they mean calling to attention the socioeconomic inequities they want to keep concealed under the guise that "we are all in this together." This guise gives cover, characteristically, to the continued "class warfare" that is steadily but surreptitiously conducted from above. Given the category of class warfare, it may be argued that all of these "interruptions" of royal narrative (in Kings and in the Gospel) are exactly practices of class warfare,

15. In the concluding doxology of Dan 6:27, the Living God is praised who "works signs and wonders." With different words we again hear witness concerning "great things" that defy the "unchanging" rule of the empire.

16. For utilization of the categories of James C. Scott to biblical texts, see Horsley, *Hidden Transcripts*.

calling attention to the discrepancies of power that must be redressed.[17] By transposing the issue of justice into the issue of faith in Luke 18:8, Jesus' teaching concerns courage, confidence, and resolve to continue the cry from below in the conviction that all the injustices perpetrated by kings, by empire, and by God are transfigurable.

There must be some irony in the fact that in Luke 18 this robust teaching on prayer is followed by another parable that culminates with the prayer, "God, be merciful to me, a sinner" (v. 13). That latter is the prayer much preferred in a church that colludes with settled power. Surely the parable in verses 3–5 is an alternative to too much "humbling." It is likely that Gehazi, who observed the "royal miracle" in its performance, would have seen the cogency of the more demanding prayer. The insistent claim of these texts is that God can indeed respond with wonders; beyond that, however, it is established that human agents can perform miracles that violate seemingly settled royal protocols. Such faith attests that justice will be done!

Bibliography

Boyce, Richard Nelson. *The Cry to God in the Old Testament*. Atlanta: Scholars, 1988.

Brodie, Thomas L. *The Crucial Bridge: The Elijah-Elisha Narrative as an Interpretive Synthesis of Genesis-Kings and a Literary Model for the Gospels*. Collegeville, MN: Liturgical, 2000.

Brueggemann, Walter. *Truth Speaks to Power: The Countercultural Nature of Scripture*. Louisville: Westminster John Knox, 2013.

Hedges, Chris. *Death of the Liberal Class*. New York: Nation Books, 2010.

Horsley, Richard A., ed. *Hidden Transcripts and the Arts of Resistance: Applying the Work of James C. Scott to Jesus and Paul*. Atlanta: Society of Biblical Literature, 2004.

Lehmann, Paul. *The Transfiguration of Politics: The Presence and Power of Jesus of Nazareth in and over Human Affairs*. New York: Harper & Row, 1975.

Noth, Martin. *The Deuteronomistic History*. JSOT Supp. 15. Sheffield: JSOT, 1981.

Scott, James C. *Domination and the Arts of Resistance: Hidden Transcripts*. New Haven: Yale University Press, 1990.

Sheppard, Gerald T. "'Enemies' and the Politics of Prayer in the Book of Psalms." In *The Bible and the Politics of Exegesis: Essays in Honor of Norman K. Gottwald on His Sixty-Fifth Birthday*. Cleveland: Pilgrim, 1991.

Walzer, Michael. *In God's Shadow: Politics in the Hebrew Bible*. New Haven: Yale University Press, 2012.

---

17. Chris Hedges has averred that "hope will come with the return of the language of class conflict and rebellion, language that has been purged from the lexicon of the liberal class." Hedges, *Death of the Liberal Class*, 17.

3

Augustine on Riches and Poverty

J. PATOUT BURNS

The post-apostolic teachers named "Fathers of the Church" worked to continue the task begun in the New Testament of discerning and explaining
the meaning and implications of the work and teaching of Jesus Christ in
a religious and social context that was significantly different from the one
in which he had lived during his brief ministry. This project became even
more complex when they were moved from the status of being (barely)
tolerated to being encouraged and then promoted in the fourth century.
An increasing number of Christian teachers were prepared by literary and
philosophical studies to engage their culture, but few of them had the political or financial experience—much less learning—that equipped them to
provide the kind of perceptive analysis of the Christian use of wealth that
they so abundantly (if not easily) did of the triune deity or the interaction
of divine and human in the Savior. Instead, their teaching about wealth was
concentrated in their sermons and focused almost exclusively on its use
and abuse. Their chief, if not exclusive, resource was attention to practice as
recorded in the scripture and enacted by their fellow Christians. What their
judgments lacked in theoretical sophistication and coherence they gained
in application to the culture and in power to move hearts through vivid
images and stories.[1]

1. The investigation reported in this essay is set in a broader historical context by the
recent publication of Peter Brown, *Through the Eye of a Needle: Wealth, the Fall of Rome,
and the Making of Christianity in the West, 350–550 AD* (Princeton: Princeton University
Press, 2012). From the same author, see as well, "Augustine and the Crisis of Wealth
in Late Antiquity," *Augustinian Studies* 36 (2005) 5–30; *Poverty and Leadership in the*

Wealth, Poverty, and Righteousness

Augustine observed that some people's actions betrayed a belief that God provided everlasting life and the higher realities associated with it but that the goods specific to earthly, temporal life were either in the control of the demons or were exclusively the results of human labor and ingenuity. Some practiced the cult of the demons and others used whatever strategies were at their disposal—moral or immoral—to secure temporal goods. These people, he explained, had failed to grasp the unity and difference of the Old and New Covenants. God promised and delivered earthly benefits to the Jews so that everyone would understand that these goods were created, controlled, and distributed by God. The story of Job clearly showed that the demons or other human beings could deprive a person of earthly goods only with God's permission.[2] Acknowledging God as the giver of earthly goods

---

Later Roman Empire, The Menahem Stern Jerusalem Lectures (Hanover, NH: University Press of New England, 2002). Other studies include the following: Steven Barbone, "Frugalitas in Saint Augustine," *Augustiniana* 44 (1994) 5–15; Geoffrey D. Dunn, "Poverty as a Social Issue in Augustine's Homilies," in *St. Augustine and His Opponents*, ed. Jane Ralls Baun et al., Studia Patristica 49 (Leuven: Peeters, 2010) 175–79; Allan D. Fitzgerald, "Almsgiving in the Works of Saint Augustine," in *Signum Pietatis: Festgabe Für Cornelius Petrus Mayer Zum 60. Geburtstag*, ed. Adolar Zumkeller, (Würzburg: Augustinus-Verlag, 1989) 445–59; Théodore Fortin, *Le droit de propriété dans Saint Augustin* (Caen: Vve A. Domin, 1906); Richard Klein, "Arm und Reich. Auskünfte und Stellungnahmen Augustins zur Sozialstruktur der Gemeinden in den neuen Predigten," in *Augustin prédicateur, 395–411*, ed. Goulven Madec, Collection des études augustiniennes 159 (Paris: Institut d'études augustiniennes, 1998) 481–91; Claude Lepelley, "La lutte en faveur des pauvres: observations sur l'action sociale de saint Augustin dans la région d'Hippone," in *Augustinus afer: Saint Augustin, africanité et universalité*, ed. Pierre-Yves Fux et al., Paradosis 45 (Fribourg: Éditions universitaires, 2003) 95–107; Claude Lepelley, "Facing Wealth and Poverty: Defining Augustine's Social Doctrine," *Augustinian Studies* 38 (2007) 1–17; David J. MacQueen, "St. Augustine's Concept of Property Ownership," *Recherches augustiniennes et patristiques* 8 (1975) 187–229; Boniface Ramsey, "Almsgiving in the Latin Church: The Late Fourth and Early Fifth Centuries," *Theological Studies* 43 (1982) 226–59; Boniface Ramsey, "Christian Attitudes to Poverty and Wealth," in *Early Christianity: Origins and Evolution to AD 600*, ed. W. H. C. Frend and Ian Hazlett (Nashville: Abingdon, 1991) 256–65; Jean Rougé, "Aspects de la pauvreté et de ses remèdes aux IVe-Ve siècles," in *Atti dell'Accademia Romanistica Costantiniana, VIII Convegno Internationale*, ed. G. Crifò and S. Giglio (Perugia: Libreria Universitaria, 1990) 227–48; Rebecca H. Weaver, "Wealth and Poverty in the Early Church," *Interpretation: A Journal of Bible and Theology* 41 (1987) 368–81; Richard Damian Finn, *Almsgiving in the Later Roman Empire: Christian Promotion and Practice (313–450)* (Oxford: Oxford University Press, 2006).

2. *Psal.* 34.1.7, 26.2.5, 73.2.

was appropriate but seeking them from the demons was wrong.[3] However, desiring and seeking earthly goods, even from God, could betray a failure to appreciate the better and more lasting gifts of the spiritual realm. In developing a figurative interpretation of the two hands of the bridegroom in Canticle 2:6, Augustine explained that the left hand was placed under the head of the bride, in which Christian faith resides, and the right hand over it. That left hand represented the temporal goods that provide consolation during earthly life but were themselves neither the foundation of happiness nor even a protection for faith. The right hand represented the lasting goods of eternal life that ought to be preferred and sought.[4]

Preaching on the scriptures, especially the Psalms, gave Augustine many opportunities to teach about wealth and poverty. When the parable of the beggar Lazarus and the rich man who ignored his misery (Luke 16:19–31) was read out in the Christian assembly, the indigent and beggars present nodded in satisfaction at the reversal of roles: they identified with Lazarus and claimed the promise of a glorious future. The wealthy, in contrast, feared future condemnation because of the benefits they were enjoying on earth. Augustine challenged both the false assurance and the anxiety that interpretation aroused. The parable was not a judgment in favor of the poor and against the rich, he insisted. How could Christ have been favoring the poor and condemning the rich by placing the beggar in the bosom of Abraham, whom the scriptures described as a very wealthy man? Indeed, by resenting the rich, the poor people in the congregation might offend Abraham and provoke his rejection of them. The parable clearly showed, Augustine explained, that the beggar was rewarded for the humility, piety, trust, and obedience to God that he shared with Abraham; the rich man was condemned for trusting in his wealth and refusing to care for the beggar at his gate. The judgment of Christ, he concluded, was based not on the wealth and indigence of the two neighbors but on the righteousness and humility of the beggar and on the injustice and self-assurance of the rich man.[5] Augustine buttressed this interpretation by appealing to the story of Job: owning earthly goods and enjoying temporal happiness had not made him an evil man. Though Job's true goodness was hidden from both demons and humans, God knew it and allowed him to be stripped of his

---

3. *Psal.* 35.7, 62.7.

4. *Psal.* 62.10, 120.8–9.

5. *Serm.* 14.2,5, 178.3; *Serm.* Denis 21(15A).5; *Serm.* Lamb. 24(20A).9; *Serm.* Mai 13(113B).2,4; *Psal.* 51.14–15, 85.3.

property to manifest his piety.[6] Abraham similarly demonstrated his devotion when he obediently offered to God that son whom he had sought and received as heir of his property.[7] By declining to take wealth for himself, therefore, Christ showed its irrelevance to righteousness, not that it was an evil to be avoided.[8]

Some passages in the Psalms required special attention because they seemed to show a divine preference for the poor or to present riches as a reward for upright living. Augustine's strategy for bringing such texts into line with his teaching on riches and poverty can be grasped through some examples. The psalmist (Ps 86:1) pleaded for God's help on the grounds of being poor and needy. This did not mean, Augustine contended, that God would not heed the prayer of the wealthy who, either by birth or through business, had gold, large households, and plantations. As long as they followed the directive of Paul (to whom he attributed the letters to Timothy and Titus) not to think too highly of themselves or to trust in earthly goods, their wealth was not held against them. God distinguished people on the basis of pride and humility, he insisted, rather than riches and poverty.[9] Similarly, Augustine challenged the psalmist's claim never to have seen, during a long life, the righteous in need or their children begging for bread (Ps 37:25). The scriptural statement should be accepted as true, he observed, but only as testimony to the speaker's inattentiveness or very limited experience. The scripture recounted both Abraham and Isaac migrating to avoid famine and Paul claiming to have experienced hunger and need in his apostolic work.[10]

The promise of earthly blessings—for example, a fruitful wife and many children around an abundant table—to all who feared God and walked the right way (Ps 128) proved a greater interpretative challenge. This assertion that God always gave earthly rewards to the virtuous did not allow exemptions and alternative rewards for those who renounced family and property to follow Christ. They could not claim that they had been promised a heavenly reward in place of this earthly one. More to the point, most poor Christians, and even the martyrs, would have to think that they had somehow gone astray, since they either did not receive or had

---

6. *Serm.* Denis 21(15A).6; *Psal.* 120.8.

7. *Psal.* 85:3.

8. *Psal.* 53:3.

9. *Psal.* 85:3.

10. *Psal.* 36.3.1.

to abandon such goods. Because Augustine preached on this psalm on the very day that his community was celebrating the feast of Felix of Nola, a renunciant and martyr, he could not overlook the conflict between this text and the counsels of Christ. Although it did not deny rewards in the future life, this psalm promised wealth and fertility before death as a sign of and reward for piety. Augustine rescued the meaning of the text by exploiting a grammatical shift—from the plural, "blessed are all," to a singular form, "you will eat," and "your wife"—that continued through the whole list of blessings. He was thus able to refer the promises made in the singular to Christ in identity with his ecclesial body rather than continuing a plural reference to individual Christians (or Jews). He then applied the rewards to the enjoyments of the heavenly rather than the earthly Jerusalem, arguing that the blessings should be interpreted allegorically as heavenly and spiritual rather than earthly and corporeal.[11] Thus, in these and other instances Augustine steadfastly refused to credit any correlation between wealth or poverty and righteousness or unrighteousness. He affirmed that God bestowed earthly blessings but insisted that these signified neither divine approval nor disapproval, that they anticipated neither eternal rewards nor punishments.

Augustine taught, then, that God was the source of all the resources and enjoyments necessary and useful for temporal, earthly life; God gave them and God allowed them to be taken away—by demons or other humans. God sometimes granted and sometimes denied petitions for these "left-hand" benefits (Cant 2:6). In contrast, God always called Christians to the spiritual and lasting goods that were represented by the right hand of the bridegroom.[12]

Augustine observed that God not only allowed the evil to prosper but regularly withheld or invited Christians to renounce the earthly benefits of wealth and children. This, he explained, clearly demonstrated that such things were less valuable and should be subordinated to the spiritual goods that God reserved for the good alone.[13] Christ had pointed out that God provided sun and rain to both the good and the evil (Matt 5:45); Augustine called attention to all the good things that followed from sun and rain and thus were given indiscriminately.[14] This divine liberality, he argued,

11. *Psal.* 127.1–5,10–16.
12. *Psal.* 26.2.5, 34.1.7, 120.9.
13. *Psal.* 51.16, 73.2–3.
14. *Psal.* 62.14.

was intended to discourage people from either accepting or rejecting the gospel for the sake of earthly goods. If God gave benefits only to the good, then the evil would be drawn to Christianity for the sake of attaining them; if God gave riches only to the evil, then the weak would be discouraged from converting and persevering in good. By granting and denying bodily things without regard to goodness and piety, God taught Christians that such goods were consolations that supported their earthly journey but that they should prefer the eternal goods that the evil would never share.[15]

Seeking earthly goods as rewards or signs of approval from God, Augustine argued, could place Christians in danger of falling away from their faith. Seeing the evil prosper could lead to the judgment that God does not judge justly, that God rewards the evil and punishes the good. It would raise questions especially for those who suffered loss as a consequence of obeying God.[16] The promises of earthly rewards that God made to Israel seem to have led to just these sorts of problems. When they failed to obey God, the Israelites suffered losses that the idolaters of the nations escaped. Some, but not all, came to understand that they should seek higher goods from God. The Jewish leaders repudiated Christ and sought his death in a vain attempt to preserve their nation.[17] Christians could be subject to the same temptation: when they lost the temporal goods they thought God was offering them, they might judge that God had deserted them and abandon their faith.[18] Thus, Christ discouraged his followers from desiring and seeking these temporary goods. Prosperity during earthly life was not promised to Christians, Augustine concluded; their rest and happiness belonged to life at the end of the age. They should give thanks for earthly goods and use them well, but their hope should be set on the permanent happiness promised in the future.[19]

The conversion Augustine was urging was illustrated in his explanation of Ps 73, where he tracked the progress of the psalmist from envy at the prosperity of the wicked toward hope and desire for God alone. The evil claimed that God did not care what they did, and the good feared that their fidelity and obedience had been vain and foolish. Further reflection brought the psalmist to the insight that evil people were deceptive and that

15. *Psal.* 66.2–3.
16. *Psal.* 35.7, 53.3, 73.1, 72.9, 79.14; *Serm.* Denis 21(15A).2.
17. *Psal.* 72.6, 73.3.
18. *Psal.* 90.17.
19. *Psal.* 48.2.1–6, 62.6, 91.1.

God's response was to beguile them with riches. At the end of life they would awake, like a beggar dreaming of abundance, to find themselves empty and abandoned. The obedient, in contrast, should recognize that to desire and seek earthly blessings, even as rewards from God, was to act like an irrational animal. To love and honor God for any other reward was to fail to love God truly.[20] True fidelity, then, was to desire and hope for God alone as one's happiness. One might receive and enjoy earthly goods as gifts from God, but one must never place trust or hope in the possession of earthly goods.

In his sermons and spoken commentaries on scripture, Augustine developed the teaching that earthly blessings were good but dangerous. Riches could lead to pride and self-satisfaction, to ignoring the human condition, and to neglecting one's responsibilities to others. Avarice, the love and desire for riches, was a more fundamental danger that afflicted rich and poor alike (1 Tim 6:9–10).

Often, Augustine distinguished earthly and heavenly goods as temporary and lasting. Earthly possessions were like an inn at which a traveler stayed but soon left for the use of another; they were not like the house in which a person made a permanent dwelling.[21] Like the poor who dreamed of wealth and awoke to their habitual deprivation, the rich would find themselves awakening at death to destitution because all their property had to be left behind on earth.[22] The Pauline text of 1 Tim 6:17 characterized riches as uncertain—which Augustine illustrated by noting that coins were appropriately round because money would not stand up on its own.[23] Only a foolish person would love and trust things that could not last and were easily lost, he concluded.

In other instances, however, Augustine distinguished bodily goods as being difficult to share. Only one person at a time could own a field or a house. More generally, he assumed that the total wealth available to human beings could not be increased. As a result, one person gained only by another's loss. The full purse one found by accident on the street had been lost by another. Every buyer required a seller, often one pressed by poverty or debt and reluctant to lose possession. One person inherited only on the death of another; one rose in wealth and honor only by another's decline.

20. *Psal.* 72.26, CCL 39:999.17–1000.30.
21. *Serm.* 14.6; *Psal.*34.1.6.
22. *Serm.* 345.1.
23. *Psal.* 83.3.

To desire earthly riches and status was to seek goods that could be acquired only by depriving others of them. How could one pray to God for the gift of wealth, then, when that would mean poverty for another? Thus Augustine compared the economic system to a bitter sea in which fish grew only by eating other fish. Being caught in the net of Christ—and then brought to shore—was thus a protection and liberation from this savage competition.[24]

Christian Forms of Life

In affirming that God was the source of earthly goods and had promised them as a reward for fidelity in the Old Testament, Augustine had to deal with the New Testament passages that specified different ways for Christians to hold and use property. In Matt 19:16–30, Christ invited a rich young man attempting to secure eternal life to distribute his property to the poor and become a disciple. When he refused, Christ advised his disciples that those attached to their wealth would find great difficulty in entering salvation. In Acts 4:32–35, the Jerusalem community was described as sharing goods and living from a common fund. In 1 Tim 6, the Pauline writer gave advice to Christians who retained their property. Augustine accepted and encouraged a way of dealing with property based on each of these three texts. In preaching to his congregation, as might have been expected, most of his attention focused on the application of the general principles for property owning articulated in the Pauline text.

Augustine clearly affirmed renunciation of wealth as a way of perfection to which Christ invited his disciples. Some Christians did sell their goods and give them to the poor, he reported, accepting with Christ's help the invitation that the rich young man had refused.[25] For the nobility, this often meant abandoning social status and political aspirations in order to live in a simpler way, gradually disposing of vast fortunes.[26] Melania the Younger and her husband Pinian, who were resident in Numidia, near Thagaste, for a period after the sacking of Rome in 410, were in the process of disbursing their combined fortunes. They visited Hippo Regius, where Augustine's congregation attempted to force Pinian to accept ordination as a presbyter of their church. Augustine managed to block the ordination; Melania and Pinian found a way to get themselves out of town. Augustine

24. *Serm.* 32.21, 239.5; *Psal.* 39.28, 64.9.
25. *Psal.* 43.25, 145.8.
26. *Psal.* 149.15.

had to defend his congregation against charges of being more interested in the couple's benefactions than their service of Christ.[27] Augustine had regular correspondence with Paulinus, who had abandoned his senatorial station to devote his energies and resources to the shrine of Felix in Nola, where he was made bishop.

Jesus' promise in Matt 19:27–28 convinced Augustine that not only the original apostles of Jesus but Paul and, indeed, all who had abandoned their property to follow Christ would sit on thrones with him to judge the nations. The angels joining them in judgment would be those who had announced the gospel, beginning with John the Baptist.[28] Occasionally, however, he challenged the assumption that renunciation of possessions brought a person to the fullness of Christian perfection. Christ had promised heavenly treasure and eternal life, he argued, only to those who actually followed him in his humility and suffering: giving up one's property was not enough. He reminded the congregation that after abandoning personal possessions, one of the disciples had betrayed Jesus and another had denied him. To this he added Paul's assertion that distributing his goods to the poor—and even handing his body over to burning—would profit nothing in the absence of charity (1 Cor 13:3).[29] Some Christians, Augustine recalled, had left all for Christ, assuming that this achievement would guarantee their salvation, only to fall in times of persecution because they trusted in themselves.[30] Giving up property, then, was a step toward a closer following of Christ but was not equivalent to giving one's life in public confession.

A second form of renunciation of goods developed into the communal life of monasticism. Its foundation was in the practice of the Jerusalem church of selling property and pooling the proceeds into a common fund, from which the needs of all members were supplied (Acts 4:32–35). Following the instructions given in Athanasius's *Life of Antony* and models he discovered in Milan, Augustine had originally attempted such a form of common life in Italy and then again upon his return to Africa.[31] With the support of Bishop Valerius, he succeeded in establishing a monastery on the grounds of the church in Hippo. This community became a seedbed for the spread of the monastic movement in Africa. Augustine himself wrote

27. *Ep.* 124–26.
28. *Serm.* 351.8.
29. *Serm.* 142.3,14, 345.6.
30. *Psal.* 90.1.9.
31. *Conf.* 6.14.24; *Serm.* 356.2.

rules for the governance of both male and female communities who lived from a common fund. Upon becoming bishop, he established such a community for his clergy in Hippo.[32]

Augustine explained that the goal of this system was to eliminate the conflict and competition between people to which private property could give rise. Those who held goods in common shared a claim on the whole, in the same way that every person had equal access to the light of the sun and the use of the air.[33] The participants were called monks not because they lived alone—which they did not—but because they all formed one person, having one heart and one soul in their many bodies.[34] In this, their community was a manifestation of the power of charity—the gift and operation of the Holy Spirit—to unite Christians into the body of Christ.[35] When the poor chose this course of action, their virtue was not to be discounted and dismissed because they had so little to abandon. Instead, they were to be praised for renouncing the desire for wealth that afflicted everyone.[36]

Within families, Augustine encouraged heirs to hold an estate in common rather than dividing it into individually owned shares. In preaching on Luke 12:13–15, he explained that Christ refused to force a division of an inheritance between two brothers because he opposed the avarice that preferred private to shared property.[37] In another sermon on the same text, he explained that Christ urged the petitioner to avoid all avarice, even the desire for what was rightfully his own.[38]

Augustine found significant values in the renunciation of private ownership and the communal use of property. The practice directly attacked the avarice and the love of wealth as a basis for social status that he found condemned in 1 Tim 6. It fostered the unity of hearts and souls that he identified as the effect of divine love or charity among Christians. He would identify the sharing of income—rather than property—among other Christians as an imitation of this practice and virtue.

32. *Serm.* 354.2.

33. *Psal.* 131.5.

34. *Psal.* 132.6.

35. *Serm.* Dolb. 26.48.

36. *Psal.* 103.3; *Serm.* Denis 17.2; *Serm.* Dolb. 22.3. This problem is more fully discussed in *De opera monachorum.*

37. *Serm.* Lamb. 5(107A).1.

38. *Serm.* 107.2–5.

Most Christians to whom Augustine preached maintained their wealth and social status, attempting to follow the commandments of Christ.[39] He urged them to follow the guidance of 1 Tim 6:17–19, using their resources for good works rather than personal aggrandizement.[40] Some were content with their own goods and refrained from stealing and impoverishing their neighbors.[41] Others supported the renunciants by endowing their communities with churches, houses, gardens, and fields.[42] Most gave at least some of their income to the poor. They could not presume, he warned, that avoiding serious sin would not require them either to suffer loss of property or to miss opportunities for gain. During past periods of persecution, he recalled, many had been called to face and make this renunciation. Even in the course of doing business, Augustine reminded his congregation, maintaining their practice of justice would often require Christians to make such a sacrifice. In extreme cases, their very lives would be in danger.[43] Some, unfortunately, were so attached to their property or desirous of attaining wealth that they preferred to sin rather than to accept any financial setback.[44]

Those with little property and financial security were no less in danger from their desire for wealth than the rich were from its possession, Augustine insisted. Once the rich young man had refused the invitation to abandon his property (Matt 19:22), Christ turned to his disciples and warned that it would be very difficult for the wealthy to enter the kingdom of heaven—comparing their passage into beatitude to that of a camel through "the eye of a needle." The disciples responded in astonishment: would anyone be saved (Matt 19:24–25)? Augustine drew out with some care the implications of this exchange. In Christ's time, as in his own, the rich were a small part of the total population and poor people were far more numerous. If Christ's reference had been to those who actually held wealth, then many would seem to have been available for salvation. In fact, he explained, the disciples were themselves far from rich and had understood correctly that Christ's warning was directed not only at those actually rich but at all who were filled with avarice and wanted what the rich alone

39. *Psal.* 149.15.
40. *Psal.* 136.13–14.
41. *Serm.* 85.1.
42. *Psal.* 103.3.16.
43. *Serm.* Denis 17.5.
44. *Psal.* 43.25.

had. For this reason, the disciples reacted in astonishment: how could anyone be saved? When Christ and the psalmist blessed and appreciated the poor, Augustine concluded, they intended not the avaricious and resentful indigent but the poor in spirit who humbly placed their trust in God. To these "poor" belonged the kingdom of heaven. Thus, neither the wealthy who oppressed the indigent nor the deprived who hungered for wealth would enter the kingdom. The poor, Augustine insisted, must not trust in their indigence any more than the rich in their abundance.[45] The Pauline teaching was even more specific: the poor must place their trust in God and be satisfied with adequate food and clothing. They must not seek or desire to become rich, powerful, and recognized (1 Tim 6:6–10).[46]

Managing Wealth

Both rich and poor Christians were in danger of thinking that wealth provided the means of a true and happy life. Those who actually enjoyed possessions might place their trust in them and thereby not only neglect the divine giver but accept the cultural bias that they were more important and valuable than others.[47] Augustine objected to the popular saying, "Only the rich really live."[48] He pointed to the uncertainty and instability of earthly possessions; people could neither fully secure them for their own use nor guarantee that they actually would pass to their intended heirs. God alone could not be lost unwillingly and thus was the sure source of happiness.[49]

All earthly goods had "worms" hidden within them that could spoil their enjoyment and value. Apples, pears, beans, and wheat, for example, each had its own pest. Augustine identified the "worm" of riches as pride. Wealth was like a nest in which excessive self-regard was nurtured and grew; even worse, it would never fly away.[50] Wealth was, of course, relative; the poor also might think too well of themselves. A beggar with a few coins to jingle could be more puffed up than the richest senator;[51] impoverished

---

45. *Serm.* Dolb. 5.11; *Serm.* 85.2; *Psal.* 51.14–15.
46. *Serm.* 39.2–3, 85.6; *Serm.* Denis 16.3; *Serm.* Morin 11.3.
47. *Serm.* 346.1, 36.5; *Psal* 51.15.
48. *Serm.* 345.1; *Psal.* 48.1.10.
49. *Serm.* 36.5, 85.3, 177.8; *Serm.* Dolb. 5(114B*).13; *Serm.* Morin 11.4.
50. *Serm.* 39.4, 61.10, 177.7; *Serm.* Morin 11(53A).4; *Psal.* 136.13.
51. *Psal.* 48.1.3.

clients boasted of a powerful patron.[52] In general, however, people mocked such pretensions and cut the poor down to size; the rich, in contrast, they admired and flattered.[53] The greater the possessions and the social status, then, the more a person was in danger of being puffed up; though apparently great and imposing, these people were actually hollow and, consequently, easily toppled into sin.[54]

Thus, Augustine followed Matt 5:3 in valuing poverty of spirit, based upon humility and trust in God, rather than modesty of financial resource and social status. He insisted that the rich should recognize that their possessions were both uncertain and a potential impediment to their salvation. The poor should let indigence prevent their being inflated by some small advantage over their fellows. Both should place all their trust in God.[55] To be counted among the poor to whom the divine promises were made, both the wealthy and the impoverished had to set their hope on God and avoid pride.[56] These poor would enter the kingdom of heaven through the eye of the needle.[57]

Many considerations were offered to the wealthy by Augustine to help them overcome the temptation to consider themselves better than the less advantaged. They should acknowledge the poor as fellow humans and even treat them as members of their households.[58] They must never forget that they too shared the human condition as children of Adam and Eve. They possessed nothing in the womb and brought nothing into the world. When stripped of their ornaments and finery, they were indistinguishable from anyone else. They would die and leave all their property behind. Their bodies would rot into common dust, though perhaps a little more decorously because of the spices in which they were wrapped. Even those set above others in society, those who ruled a household with coercive force, could be protected from pride by remembering that they shared the human situation of their subjects.[59]

---

52. *Psal.* 93.7.

53. *Serm.* 14.2.

54. *Psal.* 146.16; P 48.1.3; *Serm.* 36.2.

55. *Psal.* 72.26, 93.7, 131.26, 132.4.

56. *Psal.* 85.3.

57. *Serm.* Dolb. 5.8–13.

58. *Serm.* 36.5; *Psal.* 72.26.

59. *Serm.* 177.7; *Serm.* Dolb. 5.12; *Psal.* 72.13.

By using the Pauline exhortations of 1 Tim 6, Augustine developed a teaching that focused on interior dispositions of detachment from wealth and could be applied to all Christians: renunciants, monks, and householders, rich and poor. He then challenged those who maintained property to use it in ways that demonstrated their humility and their trust in God. Both rich and poor could accept earthly blessings as resources to be used; God was for enjoyment.[60] The Pauline text Augustine was following (1 Tim 6:8, 18) advised the poor to be content with food and clothing.[61] It commanded the rich to do good deeds liberally and generously, exploiting the power and freedom of action that the poor did not enjoy.[62]

If the wealthy were not going to sell all their property and give the proceeds to the poor, then how much should they give? The actual amount was not as important as the recognition that the sharing of wealth was a duty. All of it had been received from God, to whom the whole creation belonged as the property of a slave belonged to the master.[63] People should keep what they needed, Augustine conceded, indeed they might keep more than they actually needed. He recalled that the scribes and Pharisees gave a tenth and Christ insisted that Christians had to surpass them in righteousness to enter the kingdom (Matt 5:20). Still, the poor would accept whatever was offered.[64] In a tone that might have been slightly mocking, he suggested that the poor should not be too harsh in judging the wealthy. The rich were not as strong as the poor; they had to eat finer and more expensive food. Because of their delicate constitutions, they would become sick on a diet of the rough food that was all the poor could afford. As long as they also provided food for the poor, he urged, let them dine as they were accustomed. Everyone did not have to eat the same kind of food—at least not until famine forced it upon them. If the rich were not allowed to look down on the poor because they had to beg, neither should the poor despise the rich because they were frail.[65]

The rich, Augustine recognized, would have to hold reserves against calamities and failures that could come in the future. The actual need, however, could be difficult to anticipate. The level of a person's trust in God

60. *Serm.* 177.8.

61. *Serm.* 39.2–3, 85.6; *Serm.* Denis 16.3; *Serm.* Morin 11.3.

62. *Serm.* 36.6, 177.10; *Serm.* Morin 12.4.

63. *Psal.* 49.13,15,17.

64. *Serm.* 85.5.

65. *Serm.* 61.12.

inevitably entered the estimation. Even if all else were lost, a person would want to be sure that God had not been alienated.[66] The issue in making this decision was the kind of life a person really was striving to attain and to maintain.[67] The mortal life that was supported by earthly goods was unstable, ever changing, and quickly over. Happiness was to be found only in a future, true life.[68] An appreciation of that future life, then, was necessary to set a true value on the goods of earthly life.[69]

Still, Augustine cautioned, people should make provision not only for their children but for themselves as well. To hold back from the needy was to deprive themselves of the future use of their wealth.[70] The only way to secure the goods of earthly life and to be sure that they would be available when they were needed most was to give them away, in hope of receiving them back after death.[71] When people died, they would certainly lose all the goods that they had struggled to acquire and had retained. Both Christ, in his invitation to distribute possessions to the poor, and Paul, in his exhortation to use them for good works, promised treasure in the future heavenly life. Augustine concluded that the rich were being offered an opportunity to secure resources for themselves by sharing them with the poor. In this way, the earthly goods they could hold only temporarily would be transformed into a permanent possession.[72] In heaven, wealth would be safe from rot and thieves.[73] Augustine would later elaborate an explanation of this exchange in his exhortations to almsgiving. In his sermons on wealth, Augustine offered two analogies. Merchants often used a contract that allowed them to pay money in one place and have wheat, oil, or some other commodity delivered in another part of the world.[74] Closer to home, he observed that in the wintertime the sower tossed away grain as seed that had been grown and harvested with great labor only months before. He entrusted to the earth what he could either eat or sell, in hopes of harvesting much more during the summer. Should not the Christian entrust goods to God who

---

66. *Serm.* 177.11.

67. *Serm.* 36.6, 39.5, 61.11, 177.10, 346.1.

68. *Serm.* 346.1; *Serm.* Morin 11.5; *Io. Eu.* 22.3.

69. *Psal.* 131.26.

70. *Psal.* 48.1.14, 131.19.

71. *Serm.* 85.4.

72. *Serm.* 38.7, 61.11, 85.4, 389.4; *Psal.* 48.1.9.

73. *Serm.* Lamb. 2.

74. *Serm.* 177.10; *Psal.* 48.1.9, 132.4.

would return them in a lasting form?[75] Placing their wealth in heaven by giving it to Christ would also fix the hearts of the rich on the future life and protect them from the attractions of honor and status in earthly society.[76]

Householders might impose a kind of tax on themselves, setting aside funds for distribution to the poor. They should budget for the needs of the household and then establish a separate fund for the poor so that they did not feel they were depriving their own dependents to care for others.[77]

Although Augustine insisted that riches were not themselves evil, he preached against the love of wealth and the desire to acquire it. A person might have been wealthy before becoming Christian or might have become rich by inheritance, gift, or business once Christian. Neither condition violated the conscience, as long as the property was freely given or sold, righteousness was not bartered away in exchange, and the riches did not result in pride or become the object of trust.[78] The poor, of course, were subject to the same temptation to love and desire wealth, as Paul warned (1 Tim 6:6–10). The truly poor, those whom Christ recognized as the poor in spirit, were to be found among both the wealthy and the destitute: they were free of avarice.[79]

Augustine taught that restraint in the acquisition and use of money was like faithful sexual practice within marriage: a proper and laudatory use of a good whose abandonment was better and deserving of greater reward.[80]

Sharing Wealth

The principal form of good work performed on the basis of property and wealth was identified as almsgiving. Augustine extended the practice to the poor as well as the rich and identified different values that it served and functions that it performed within the community.

In his sermons and expositions of the scriptures, Augustine developed a doctrine of the church as the social body of Christ and of Christians as the members of that body. He used a broad range of texts from the New

75. *Serm.* Morin 11.5.

76. *Serm.* 38.7; *Psal.* 36.3.8, 48.2.1.

77. *Psal.* 146.17.

78. *Serm.* 39.3–4; *Serm.* Morin 11(53A).4, 12(25A).2.

79. *Serm.* 14.

80. *Psal.* 147.4.

Testament and applied the doctrine to the interpretation of the Old Testament, particularly the Psalms. Two of the texts he used, the account of the final judgment in Matt 25:34–46 and the risen Christ's confrontation of Paul in Acts 9:3–8, were directly and immediately applicable for interpreting the giving of alms and other services. Because Christ had clearly identified himself with Christians, both in being persecuted and in receiving services, Augustine assigned a religious value to these actions that could not be applied to similar gifts and services provided to non-Christians.

Augustine explained that although Christ was now risen and safely in heaven, his identification with the members of his ecclesial body meant that he continued to need assistance on earth. Christ thereby made himself available to be served in the Christian poor and thus offered those who responded the opportunity to win salvation.[81] Christ could, of course, have cared for his poor members directly, but he preferred that they be served by his others members, who also benefitted from the exchange. The best illustration was the feeding of Elijah first by the crow, which received no benefit, and then by the widow, who was preserved from famine by her service. When recognized by Christian faith, therefore, the recipient was a minister bestowing a greater blessing on the giver of alms.[82] Christ, Augustine observed, had freely taken on poverty and identified with the poor so that Christians might exercise generosity toward God. Those who recognized him and kept faith with him, who were not ashamed of his poverty, would enjoy the heavenly goods that were his.[83]

Using the identification of Christ with his members as a foundation for the giving of alms made the recipient's relationship to Christ relevant to the appropriateness of the gift. Augustine found a clarifying parallel to Matt 25:40 in Matt 10:41–42 where Jesus promised rewards to those who assisted his disciples when they were sent to preach the gospel. There Christ specified that receiving a prophet or righteous person because of that role or status would bring to the benefactor the reward of being a prophet or righteous. Similarly, the cup of cold water given because of discipleship would not go unrewarded. To this text, Augustine added one first found in the *Didache* (1.6) that he regarded as authoritative: "Let your alms sweat in your hand until you find a just person to whom you can give them."

81. *Serm.* 9.21, 25.8, 38.8, 86.3.3, 206.2, 236.3, 239.4.4–6.7; *Serm.* Mai 13(113B).4; *Serm.* Lamb. 4(359A).11; *Psal.* 36.3.6.

82. *Serm.* 103.2, 239.3–4, 277.1.

83. *Serm.* 41.6–7, 389.6.

Christians had a special responsibility to seek out the just and the servants of Christ in order to care for their needs. Beggars would approach and ask for relief, but Christ's disciples often preferred to suffer in silence. Discovering and supporting these disciples was a special service to Christ and made the donor share in their good works and holy lives.[84]

The principle of supporting Christ in the poor did not mean that alms should be given only to those who could be identified as righteous. As one could support a prophet without recognizing the prophecy and thereby fail to gain the special reward, so a Christian could and even should give to a sinner on the basis of need alone, without thereby approving and sharing the guilt of the sin. The beggar was first a human being and on that basis an appropriate object of mercy. Giving to gladiators, actors, fortune-tellers, and prostitutes should be questioned: would the donation be made if its recipients were not so employed? To receive a sinner as a sinner earned no reward. In fact, donors had some obligation to rebuke the sin itself, particularly if the recipient was under their power or influence.[85]

One might object, Augustine acknowledged, that giving to sinners was acting against the intention of God by alleviating the very punishment being visited upon their sin. Not so, he replied. Christ commanded that Christians should love their enemies and do good to those who hated them (Matt 5:44). He willingly accepted even vinegar to quench his thirst from one who was mocking him as he died; so too, Christians should not hold back from helping enemies—their own or God's.[86] Proverbs 25:21–22 advised that God would reward the person who gave food and drink to an enemy. Paul, in Gal 6:9–10, recommended special generosity toward fellow Christians but insisted that alms should be given not only to the just but to sinners and persecutors as well. The sin should be rebuked to make clear that the Christian was supporting but not approving the sinner.[87]

Although Christians had a special responsibility to seek out and assist those striving to follow and to serve Christ, they should be generous to anyone in need. Their being too careful with alms might result in depriving the worthy in order to avoid the unworthy, since human hearts were so difficult to judge. If they had an obligation to known enemies, then why not to those of whom they were uncertain? If the sower was too careful with his

---

84. *Psal.* 102.12–13, 103.3.10, 146.17.

85. *Psal.* 102.13–14.

86. *Serm.* 41.7.

87. *Serm.* Lamb. 28(164A).1–4.

seed in the wintertime, trying to make sure that none of it was wasted on the road or on rocky soil, then he would go hungry at the summer harvest.[88]

In practice, the congregation at Hippo seems to have extended its gifts of financial and material support to Roman traditionalists, Jews, and Christian heretics, all of whom were ready to accept the gifts though they had no intention of sharing the faith.[89] A collection for the poor seems to have been taken each Sunday. On one occasion, at the end of a sermon and thus before the dismissal of catechumens, candidates, penitents, and the curious, Augustine announced that the collection was short. The needs of the poor could not be met with what had been given that day. He urged those present to make up the difference to the beggars outside as they left the basilica.[90] On another occasion, when preaching on the wedding garment necessary for participating in the heavenly banquet, he reminded his hearers that this was a gift of God. He then suggested that winter was coming on and the poor would be in need of heavier garments. If they clothed the poor, he promised, God would clothe them in the charity represented by the wedding garment.[91]

Augustine universalized the process of giving and receiving alms; because almsgiving gave Christians access to Christ himself, he concluded that the Christian poor must be not only recipients but also givers of alms. He used two instances of Christ's teaching to justify his assertion that the indigent were also expected to care for others in need. When Jesus sent out his disciples, he promised that not even a cup of cold water given to one of his followers would go unrewarded (Matt 10:42). The specification of cold water, he argued, indicated that the donor did not have the resources to make it more palatable by heating the water.[92] The widow who contributed two small coins to the upkeep of the temple provided another example (Luke 21:1–4).[93] The poor could offer services even when they had no goods to share: to help the lame and the blind, to care for the sick, and to bury the dead. The listing of services that could be offered allowed Augustine

88. *Serm.* 41.7.; *Serm.* Lamb. 4(359A).11.

89. *Psal.* 32.3.29, 46.5.

90. *Serm.* 66.5.

91. *Psal.* 95.7.

92. *Serm.* 39.6, 47.30; *Serm.* Dolb. 26(198*).20; *Psal.* 125.12, 49.13, 111.3, 121.11, *Serm.* Lamb. 4(359A).11, 5(107A).8.

93. *Serm.* Dolb. 26(198*).20; 39.6, 47.30; *Serm.* Lamb. 1(105A).1, 4(359A).12, 5(107A).7; *Psal.* 49.13.

to include among the almsgivers both the clergy and others living from a common fund: some offered instruction, advice, or sympathy in place of funds, food, clothing, or shelter.[94] He concluded that the love exercised in giving determined the value of the gift and the reward it deserved.[95]

The Efficacy of Almsgiving

Augustine identified many roles that almsgiving played within the Christian life and the process of salvation. It was not only a means of dealing with the temptation to pride and self-sufficiency on the part of the rich but a practice in which the poor as well should engage on an appropriate scale.

As has just been noted, Augustine identified caring for the poor as one of the means of attaining the charity that was a constitutive element of salvation. In his commentaries on the First Letter of John, Augustine recalled that the Gospel of John identified the greatest work of love as dying for one's fellows. He then specified delivering them from temporal distress as the first step toward that goal, as a means of nourishing charity. A Christian unwilling to expend surplus income in coming to the rescue of another was hardly loving at all.[96]

In other contexts, almsgiving was described as lending efficacy to prayer, both for a Christian's needs and for the forgiveness of sins. The rich knock on the door of God asking for help even as the poor are banging on their own doors for food. The rich ask for the greatest of goods, God alone, who can be attained only as a gift, while the poor ask only for sustenance. As the emaciated flesh of the poor was a plea for alms, the giving of alms was itself a prayer with one's hands and life rather than with the voice alone. For the rich to refuse to give to the needy of their excess while seeking God's mercy for themselves would be, Augustine explained, like trying to reap without first sowing. Generosity toward the poor, then, was essential to any appeal to God for one's own needs. In this sense, Augustine understood sharing wealth as the Christian replacement for the animal sacrifices of Israelite practice.[97]

94. *Serm.* 91.7.9; *Psal.* 36.2.13, 125.11–13.

95. *Psal.* 121.11, 125.12, 47.30, *Serm.* Lamb. 5(107A).8.

96. *Io. Ep.* 5.12–6.1.

97. *Serm.* 88.12–13, 206.2; *Serm.* Haffner 1(350B).1 and *Serm.* Étaix 3(350C).1–2; *Psal.* 49.20.

Almsgiving as a plea for the forgiveness of sins was a well-established practice for Jews and Christians. Augustine regularly cited Christ's exhortation to "giving and forgiving" in Luke 6:37–38 to indicate these as inseparable forms of generosity extended and received. Almsgiving was the Christian form of the offering or sacrifice for sin. It was the regular means of cleansing from the nearly inevitable failures of daily life and a daily prayer for Christ's help to improve one's life.[98] For more serious sins, however, it could never substitute for repentance and reform.[99] For some reason, Augustine judged that he had to explain that alms could be given only from wealth honestly acquired. Alms given from fraud, theft, or usury could not offset that sin, particularly when the sinner was usually willing to give away only a small portion of the ill-gotten gains. Was Christ to hear the prayers of the beneficiary of the alms and to ignore the groans of the victim whose money was being dispensed?[100] If the victim was a Christian and thereby a member of Christ, how was this to play out within the judgment scenario described in Matt 25? Christ would be rewarding those who had clothed him and condemning those who ignored his nakedness. Then he would come to the person who first stripped him and later handed back a few scraps of his clothing. Such a pillager would hardly get a heavenly reward: even the flames of hell would be a mercy.[101] The graphic images of these sermons suggest that Augustine was dealing with a significant problem: the congregation must have contained a good number of predators, as well as their victims.

On the more positive side, Augustine exhorted almsgiving as a means of winning salvation by turning earthly into heavenly goods. Because of the relationship between Christ and Christians, Augustine could assert that although Christ was rich in heaven, he continued to be poor and needy on earth, where he received gifts that he would repay in heaven.[102] Augustine compared the process to a mercantile transaction through which funds and goods could be exchanged between parts of the empire. What was given or received in one port could be repaid in another.[103] Alms, then, were like a loan made to Christ in earthly goods that would then be collected

---

98. *Serm.* 9.17–18,21, 42.1, 39.6, 83.2.

99. *Serm.* 39.6.

100. *Serm.* 113.2; *Serm.* Lamb. 4(359A).13.

101. *Serm.* 178.4–5.

102. *Serm.* 18.4, 38.8–9, 345.4–5.

103. *Serm.* 390.2, 345; *Serm.* Mai 11(53A).6.

in heavenly ones. The poor in this schema were like agents for Christ who received gifts that he would return.[104] Augustine also compared the system to a complex storage facility for liquids—not unlike the cisterns of a Roman city—in which something poured into one could pass through a system of pipes and be drawn from another.[105] Christ had designed the system, and his promise that it would work could be trusted. The Christian poor, then, had a special role in the economy of salvation: they could transform temporal and earthly goods into lasting and heavenly ones; their bellies were secure storehouses; they were porters who carried things from one realm to the next.[106]

Such transactions, moreover, could be made not only for the benefit of the person making the gift but for another. Augustine considered the objection that householders had a responsibility to preserve their goods so that they could pass them to their children. Hence, they should not give alms to the poor who did not belong to their families. Augustine pointed out that this kind of excuse could be repeated endlessly from generation to generation: no one would ever heed the command of Christ. He then complicated the discussion: what should be done if one of the children died? Might the householder then send to the departed the part of the inheritance that would have been given later? Or was it to be divided among the surviving children, each of whom would then have cause to rejoice in the early death of their sibling? Should the departed not receive a rightful share? Should that portion belonging to the child not be sent ahead through the poor as a gift to Christ in the name of the deceased? The deceased had need of the patrimony and it could be sent along to follow the soul, now awaiting the judgment of Christ. Let the householder, then, make the contract for transfer of the property and deliver the funds to the child.[107] Augustine suggested another possibility for enriching the entire family: let the father adopt Christ as a son, pay out his portion of the inheritance, and thus enrich all his children by making them coheirs of Christ's fortune.[108]

Almsgiving was the one instance, Augustine explained, in which Christians were allowed to practice usury. For the most part, Christians regarded usury in lending—demanding more in return than had been

104. *Serm.* 38.9, 339.6; *Serm.* Dolb. 26(198*).4.
105. *Psal.* 38.12.
106. *Serm.* 36.9, 38.9, 60.6, 302.8, 389.3; *Serm.* Mai 11(53A).6.
107. *Serm.* 9.20, 85.11–12.
108. *Serm.* 86.13–14; *Psal.* 48.1.14.

given in the loan—as the exploitation of the misfortune of the debtor. When Christians gave to relieve the misery of another, however, Augustine suggested that they consider it a loan that Christ had signed and certified. He would repay and would gladly give far more than the member of his ecclesial body had received. A Christian creditor could count Christ as the most trustworthy of debtors; a hundred times more could be expected in return than had been advanced.[109]

Almsgiving, as Augustine presented it to his congregation, was the effective means of dealing with the uncertainty of earthly riches. The person who had earthly property was always anxious about securing it. It had to be hidden away and in the charge of a servant, but even then the wealth was either corruptible—grain or another commodity—or in danger from thieves. Many masters, he suggested, had been betrayed by servants who fled with their riches or joined and gave access to a band of plunderers. Much property was immovable—a house or farm—and had to be sold or abandoned. Even if it was secure, the owner could enjoy it for only a lifetime and then had to leave it behind.[110] Christ's advice was to move the wealth from earth to heaven where it would not only be safe under his care but would already be where the owner hoped to go. Augustine used an analogy. A person knowledgeable about grain noticed that an inexperienced friend had stored wheat underground, where it would be damp. He suggested that it ought to be moved to a higher, dryer place before it began to rot. Everyone in the congregation would have realized that the advice was good. Would it not be wise to follow the advice of Christ—who had built the world itself—to move wealth to a higher, safer place?[111] He told the story of a man of modest means who exchanged a solid gold coin for a hundred smaller ones and gave a portion to the poor. A thief, at the instigation of the devil, then stole the remainder. Instead of cursing God for allowing the loss, the victim regretted not having given away the whole sum, so that it would still be his in heaven.[112] If Christians really loved their wealth, Augustine concluded, they should be shrewd about holding onto it. By giving it to Christ's poor, they might enjoy it forever.

---

109. *Serm.* 86.3, 239.5; *Psal.* 36.3.6.
110. *Serm.* 38.8, 345.2–3, 389.4; *Serm.* Lamb. 2(335C) 8–9.
111. *Serm.* 390.1; *Psal.* 36.3.6, 48.1.9.
112. *Serm.* 389.4.

Concluding Observations

Augustine's teaching on the limitations imposed on almsgiving by a responsibility for supporting self and family was significantly different from Cyprian's urging that Christians should sell their property and contribute the proceeds to the poor without thinking about the future.

The affirmation of the goodness of wealth itself and the appeal to Abraham and Job as indications that saints could be wealthy might have been motivated by Augustine's concern with Manichaean teaching. It might also reveal a division within the community between the rich and the poor, based on the self-importance of the wealthy and the resentment of the impoverished.

In all instances, the sharing of wealth was integral to Augustine's teaching. He insisted that the renunciation of wealth was not required of all but that its sharing was essential. Riches were not evil, but the desire that made them private and unavailable to others was.

Both the sermons and the discussions of what was essential for entering the kingdom of God in *On the City of God* indicate that Augustine was faced with Christians, even within his own congregation, who stole from and defrauded others. Instead of apologizing and making restitution to their victims, at least some of them attempted to acquire forgiveness from God by giving away a portion of their ill-gotten gains to the poor.[113]

Finally, a question: might Augustine have judged that the inevitable and even necessary privatization of the goods necessary to support life in the postlapsarian world was in conflict with the demands of universal charity? Like mortality, lust, and domination, private property and disparity of wealth were both a result and an indicator of humanity's fallen condition, from which Christ would set free his elect. Christian sharing of wealth was, then, a sign of the coming of the kingdom.

113. *Ciu.* 21.22.

4

The Future of the Wesleyan Movement

JOHN B. COBB JR.

I

Doug Meeks and I share many things, and I regret that there have not been more occasions for us to work together. We have both written on economics and both of us care deeply for the human fate. He is a church theologian; and I have aspired to be one, even if that has not been my primary vocation. He has served the national church well. My efforts to do so have been more limited and much less successful. In honoring Doug, I have decided to reflect on the direction that the segment of the United Methodist Church with which I most fully identify might go in this difficult time.

I select this topic because of the intense alienation that my pastor and my friends have expressed in the aftermath of the 2012 General Conference. They love the Wesleyan spirit as they understand it and have long felt at home in the United Methodist Church. They have been proud of the denomination's Social Creed. The beginning of the alienation came when the General Conference of 1972 inserted into that creed the statement that homosexual acts are incompatible with the Christian faith. Up until that change to its text the Social Creed had been at the progressive edge of mainstream Christian thinking. That addition turned it into a weapon of oppression against many in our pews and far more in the wider society.

Our collective response has been to take what actions were still available to us to express our love for our gay brothers and sisters. My congregation joined the reconciling movement. We worked hopefully from

47

quadrennium to quadrennium to move past this judgmental legalism. We rejoiced as other denominations moved forward, thinking that in time we could join them. This time that hope seems to have been quashed. We are condemned to being part of a denomination that places law above the well-being of human beings. Instead of being in the lead in social advance, we as a global church have committed ourselves to blocking it.

In my congregation sexual orientation and sexual morality are assumed to be entirely different issues. There is no virtue in being heterosexual. Heterosexuals are called to high standards of sexual conduct. There is no virtue in being homosexual. Homosexuals are called to high standards of sexual conduct. For heterosexuals to deny sexual fulfillment to homosexuals or to punish them for seeking it is exactly the kind of judgment that Paul most passionately condemned in just that passage that homophobes like to cite in their own defense: "Therefore you have no excuse, whoever you are, when you judge others; for in passing judgment on another you condemn yourself, because you, the judge, are doing the very same things" (Rom 2:1).

I may, of course, be unfair and mistaken. Yet I am trying to give expression to a deeply felt alienation on the part of a large segment of the United Methodist people in my part of the world. For us, sexual orientation is not a moral issue. It is simply a fact. Sexual fulfillment is not a good to be allowed only to those with the majority orientation. It is a good for human beings as human beings. These are not issues for further deliberation. They are obvious truths. We rejoice that other denominations are recognizing these truths and ceasing to bicker about their sexual prejudices. They can move on to deal with the profoundly critical issues we all face in a dying civilization on a dying planet. It is hard to accept the fact that the heirs of John Wesley, the most progressive founder of any major Protestant movement, have decided to become rigidly legalistic on this important issue, largely blocking any effective voice on any other issue.

To us this denominational commitment is a denial of Jesus' gospel of love and of Paul's affirmation that we are all saved by grace. It seems to encourage a legalistic spirit in other areas as well. It seems to prevent our denomination from giving leadership on saving the world from the terrible ecological disasters toward which it is heading. How can we be faithful followers of Jesus Christ, understanding the meaning of his life, death, and resurrection through the eyes of Paul, moved and inspirited by John and Charles Wesley, and still be part of a denomination that, in our perspective, has turned in a different direction?

II

Before proceeding, however, we need to look at ourselves. Are we not being self-righteous? Are we perhaps trying to remove a speck from the eyes of others, while a beam is lodged in our own? More broadly, what is our responsibility for the ugly situation in which we now find ourselves? Let us take a broader look.

We progressive United Methodists need to recognize the depth of our collective failures. Our whole denomination is losing ground in American society, but the losses are heaviest in the most progressive sections. If "progress" means disconnecting with the people we should be serving, we can hardly blame others for disconnecting from "progress." A serious analysis of how and why this is occurring is beyond the scope of this paper, but I will hazard some generalizations.

The Wesleyan movement grew when its members understood what it offered to be supremely important. Wesley held before his hearers a picture of the authentic Christian life, the life of perfect love. He persuaded them that God called them to shape their lives in this direction and assured them that God's grace was sufficient to move them along this line. He organized people in groups that kept them seriously reflective about their personal progress and helped them move forward. They felt that nothing could be more important than this.

From the beginning there were dangers and distortions. The idea that God made some people perfect in this life did great damage. Although Wesley was remarkably free of legalism, it was always too easy to replace love with particular acts thought to express it. Sadly, instead of standing guard against these distortions, the church as a whole simply moderated its expectations.

Wesley saw this happening. His followers came mainly from the poorer rungs of society. The self-discipline he taught led many to "advance" into the middle class. That meant that they had money and were increasingly interested in its accumulation and in acquiring the good things it would buy. The tension between the love of money and the wholehearted service of God was noted by Jesus long ago. Wesley saw it at work. Methodists became middle-class and, along with that, lukewarm or half-hearted.

When a Christian's concern for economic well-being makes it impossible to be wholly committed to love of God and neighbor, what happens? Like the rich young ruler, one may observe many good rules of behavior. Alternately, one may focus on generating good emotions; or one may replace the extreme ideal of Jesus and Wesley with the wisdom of contemporary psychologists. One may even devote oneself to achieving economic justice and other good social goals. Some may combine these directions in various ways. There then remains a tension between the new, less-demanding understanding of the goal and the scriptures and hymns that promote the unqualified love of God and neighbor.

Meanwhile another development occurred. In the early days, Wesleyans shared with the general public in a naïve reading of the Bible as the word of God. This practice is not to be confused with contemporary fundamentalism, which has a strongly reactive character. Common sense played a large role, and one did not have to take everything at face value. Wesley, for example, interpreted each part of the Bible in light of the rest. On the whole, such diversity as existed in the understanding of the nature of the Bible was not seriously divisive.

However, in the nineteenth century, biblical scholarship led many, including most of the leadership of the Wesleyan movement, to recognize that the Bible is a human creation. Like all human creations, God was at work in this process. Yet the Bible as a book has all the marks of other ancient literature. This in no way means that it lacks spiritual authority, but it is not supernatural or absolute.

Progressives, by definition, allied themselves with this understanding of the Bible as a work of ancient literature. Many in the churches, and some in the academy, resisted this profound change. The Christian movement as a whole was deeply split and has remained so to this day.

There have always been some who have used the new freedom in relation to the biblical texts to advance Christian thinking and to liberate it from incredible and especially from harmful ideas. Many took the new scholarship as a weapon against "fundamentalists" and, indeed, against conservatives and pious folk generally, and they have found satisfaction in tearing down widely held assumptions and beliefs. Biblical study was taken over more and more as an academic discipline to be pursued in the value-free fashion demanded by the modern research university. Prestige went to those who dealt most critically and skeptically with the texts. Talk of God was radically separated from biblical scholarship. In other words, the study of the Bible was taken away from the church and popular use of the Bible ceased to be respectable. Seminary professors had the task of helping prospective ministers bridge this gap, but their own doctoral studies gave them little guidance in doing so. Neo-orthodoxy made a valiant effort to respond

to this dilemma, but it did not put down deep roots in the United Methodist Church. In the view of progressives, this failure was not to be deplored.

Within the Methodist Church, the healthiest and strongest response to
this range of problems was the Social Gospel. Biblical scholarship showed
that Israel's understanding of God developed over time. The prophetic
movement was the most advanced understanding to be found in the Jewish
scriptures. This focused attention on living out the covenant with God in the
way people treated one another. Economic issues played a large role. Jesus'
proclamation of the *basileia theou* was best seen as the culmination of that
movement. Our highest calling was to commit ourselves wholeheartedly
to working for the coming of what we have been accustomed to calling the
"kingdom," or what I prefer to call the "commonwealth," of God. This was
understood to be the fullest expression of the love of God and of neighbor.

Of course, this movement also had its distortions and dangers. Some
of its slogans suggested that human beings are capable of "building the
kingdom of God," thus failing to acknowledge our collective and individual
sinfulness and our utter need for grace. The Depression and World War
II made this whole emphasis seem unrealistically optimistic. Nevertheless, this expression of progressive Christianity dominated the Methodist
movement between the two world wars and gave it considerable vitality. Its
Social Creed and its participation in the wider ecumenical movement for
peace and justice were second to none.

The health of the church during that period was grounded in the Wesleyan piety that still played a deep role. Private, family, and church prayer
were central to the lives of those devoted to bringing God's kingdom to the
world. Partly for this reason, even those who understood their Wesleyan
faith in highly personal terms and disagreed with some of the political
policies the church supported were not deeply alienated. The theology of
Boston Personalism served well to keep these foci together. Although the
aim of perfection in love as treated by Wesley had been highly personal, for
him the personal had never been purely individual. The love of neighbor
called not only for helping the neighbor who was at hand but also for ending the slave trade.

I dare to claim that during those two periods, the major branches
of the Methodist movement were devoted to the "economy of salvation."
Although that phrase calls attention to a goal that far exceeds what is today understood by economics, in both periods economics in the narrow
sense was important. In the earlier period nothing was more important, or

indicative of one's progress in the movement toward perfect love, than one's use of money. In the latter period, the social justice and righteousness one sought was inextricably connected with the structure of the economy.

The real decline of the Wesleyan churches is primarily a matter of the post-World War II years. It began with the period of institutional flourishing right after World War II. This institutional flourishing resulted from the cultural climate following the war. Anti-Communism contributed to support for a vaguely Christian culture. Returning soldiers greatly appreciated the nuclear family and wanted the help of the Christian community in bringing up their children. Being a church member was socially expected. As new suburbs grew up around the cities, new churches were planted and quickly attracted members.

However, it was clear that these members did not come out of a desire for heroic virtue or to work together for justice in society. They came together for fellowship, moral encouragement, and for a wholesome context for their children. They wanted practical help and guidance with their lives. Of the earlier options in retaining some part of the Wesleyan legacy, current psychological wisdom suited the new members best. Preaching about the economy of salvation was rare. Seriously asking people to shape their use of money in the service of personal perfection in love or social justice was viewed as out of place except as the church asked for financial support from its members. During this period the church was acculturated more than ever before. That is, it responded to the felt needs of people without defining for them a different goal. Interest in the economy of salvation largely disappeared.

The consequence of this short-term success was long-term failure. Children brought up in those churches were not persuaded of the distinctive importance of what they experienced there. When they grew up and had children, they sometimes wanted them to have what they had gotten from their churches in their own childhood. Yet as adults most of them felt no special need for a church. They could find fellowship and instruction and psychological advice elsewhere, and worship seemed more of an archaic form than a central requirement of a good life.

Those who did stay with the church more out of conviction than out of habit or the remnants of social pressure were likely to be attached to its most conservative forms or else to want to continue the Social Gospel. The latter rejoiced in a succession of liberation movements. The former found these disruptive of the traditional church they loved. Since denominational

leadership was still largely in the hands of those who were heirs of the Social Gospel, the churches did respond to the demands of various groups for
full recognition and leadership participation. During this process it was
conservatives rather than progressives who were likely to feel alienated.

As long as we progressives could do so, we ran roughshod over the
conservatives. We were sure we were right in opening doors fully to ethnic
minorities and to the leadership of women, and we were glad that we could
overcome their resistance. In our self-righteousness, we did little to ease the
pain of those who did not want to change in these ways. We wrote them off.

The conservatives found it difficult to defend racism and sexism, but
eventually they had their chance. They could not affirm that race or sex was
a moral issue, but when it came to sexual "deviancy" they could—and did.
They could quote scripture against us. Since then, they have been running
roughshod over us.

I am contrasting the progressive victories of inclusion after World War
II with the progressive victories on issues of peace and justice during the
heyday of the Social Gospel. At that earlier time there was a shared Wesleyan piety that allowed for differences without breaking a sense of com-
monality. Some Wesleyans worked chiefly on issues of social justice. Others
cultivated personal relationships. The two groups could worship together
with a feeling of mutual respect. Yet when some define the heart of the
biblical message as inclusiveness and others identify Christianity with the
prejudices of secular culture and the moral rules of their childhood, there
is little that holds them together except an institutional structure. There has
been a decline of Wesleyan piety all across the board, but the decline may
be greatest among progressives. If we do have spiritual disciplines, they are
as likely to be learned from Hindus or Buddhists as from Wesley.

III

I have described what I take to be two healthy periods in our Wesleyan
heritage. There was the period in which people gathered out of the conviction that becoming perfect in love was of supreme importance. There
was the period in which believers could understand that nothing could be
more important than reshaping the world according to God's will. Followers of Wesley never thought that denominational affiliation was essential to
pursuit of these goals. Yet to participate in Wesleyan piety and to be a part
of one of the Wesleyan denominations was an excellent way of expressing

commitment to these goals. However, in the years following World War II, there has been no comparable unifying commitment.

Of course, some suppose that they need to be Christian in order to go to heaven, and the United Methodist Church is one way to meet this requisite. This continuity of belief from earlier times gives intensity to the concerns of many conservatives and lingers on, half-consciously, among others. They rightly perceive that progressives undermine this traditional idea, and they see this loss of otherworldly focus as the main reason for the decline of the church—even though it was never a distinctive part of the Wesleyan movement.

Among others who continue to be active in the church, there are some who think the church is important to the social and moral health of the nation and support it accordingly. Others find the church to be an avenue through which they can express their passion for inclusiveness, for peace, for justice, and for sustainability. Many love the biblical stories and admire Jesus and want their children to do so also. Still others find the church a supportive community of which they feel a need. Reasons like these for supporting the church do not capture the commitment of a new generation.

Many simply drift away, but others leave on principle. They suppose that if they participate in the life of the church, they are supporting beliefs that in fact they do not share. In some cases, this is simply a matter of lack of credibility. For example, one may be persuaded by a normal university education that nothing properly called "God" exists, even if one might like to believe. In other cases, the beliefs in question seem harmful. The idea that God controls everything seems incompatible with human responsibility and maturity. The belief that Jesus is the one way to God is seen as incompatible with full respect and appreciation for other religious traditions. The teachings of the church on gender and sexuality are felt to be oppressive and psychologically and sociologically harmful.

Overall, progressives are good at showing that one need not hold to incredible doctrines or exclusive and oppressive teachings in order to be a faithful participant in the life of the church. The idea of divine omnipotence is not really biblical at all. One can understand that to put Jesus at the center opens the door to appreciation and respect for the wisdom of many traditions. One can also show that legalism on sexual matters is profoundly contrary to the teaching of Jesus and Paul. Progressives are good at identifying causes to which Christians should commit themselves.

THE FUTURE OF THE WESLEYAN MOVEMENT 55

Progressives are rarely good at showing that the church rightly claims a central role in the lives of people who seem to get along quite well without it. Progressives are much better at distancing themselves from fundamentalists than at providing convincing reasons why their own children should commit themselves to the church. Their children find that they can distance themselves still further from fundamentalists by abandoning the church altogether.

IV

The most basic reason for the decline of the church is the loss of belief that being a participant in the church is truly important. In truth it has never been more important than it is today. With all the church's failures and weaknesses it continues to have an importance that it seems rarely able to articulate. Simply understanding its role in society more deeply would make the value of the church, even when it is in decay, clearer. However, I shall approach the matter from the other end. Is there a goal we could state clearly today that is of extreme importance, around which we could rally and revive the church?

I think there is. The world is heading for catastrophe. It is too late to prevent catastrophes of many sorts from occurring, but we may hope it is not too late to salvage something from the wreckage and to build something new in the ashes. The church played this role after the fall of the Roman Empire. It may not be meaningless to order our shared life as Christians so as to respond positively to the horrors that await us. Today, as in every day, we are called to work with God to "save the world" that God loves. The implications of this call are different now than they were in the period between the world wars when the Social Gospel flourished. That is, we must rethink the "economy of salvation." Much that Wesley taught about perfection in love and much that was proclaimed by those who discovered the deeply social character of the prophetic message has direct relevance to today's "economy of salvation." The need for "salvation" has never been more urgent than in our time, when the future of the human species is at stake.

To align ourselves with God's working to save the world at this time and place is, then, a matter of supreme importance. It subsumes all that can be done to achieve inclusiveness, justice, peace, and sustainability. It expresses our love of God and neighbor. It makes clear how urgently we need God's help and community with others who also seek God's help to save the world.

It is hard to think of anything more important than the salvation of the world. It is hard to think that there is any more urgent matter than finding groups of people who are willing to subordinate their quests for personal security and prosperity to the shared quest for this salvation. It is hard to imagine a better grounding for such groups and the individuals who make them up than faith in God as we have come to know God in Jesus. Such groups, grounded in this way, are surely the church. I believe that this church will bring out the best in many who will understand the radical nature and the authority of its call.

This goal can subsume both the goal of perfection in love and the goal of realizing the commonwealth of God. It will require disciplined sharing and mutual support in difficult decisions. This can best be achieved as people organize themselves into small groups of intimate and honest sharing and mutual support. Wesley would surely approve.

V

Yet is not such a program so remote from the contemporary reality of the United Methodist Church that to pursue it simply requires organizing something quite different? That may be the case. One can hardly imagine taking a typical existing congregation and turning it into groups of people wholly dedicated to working with God for the salvation of the world.

On the other hand, I hope that my description of what is needed shows how this vision flows naturally from our distinctive Wesleyan history. The Wesleyan movement has been able in the past to contain groups of this kind, and organizing new ones might have a rapidly growing effect on existing congregations. They might attract into the church some who have long ago given up on it as irrelevant to the real needs of the world. New leadership might arise from these new members that could carry the whole church forward. This is not altogether fanciful thinking—or so I suppose.

The call is for the United Methodist Church that was so deeply acculturated during the postwar years of growth and prosperity to become a systemically and self-consciously countercultural movement. The culture is oriented to Mammon. Jesus said directly and explicitly that we cannot serve both God and Mammon. For decades now we have tried to do so. The effort has failed, as both Jesus and Wesley clearly predicted. The worship of

Mammon is destroying the habitability of the planet. Few communities or institutions today seriously attempt to repudiate the worship of Mammon and to serve only God. If Christians will not respond to this call, where can the world turn for leadership? Where can we even find a discussion of "the economy of salvation"?

Where can we begin in creating such a discussion and bringing into being communities that seek to live by it? I am asking specifically about a church that professes to follow Jesus in a way inspired by Wesley.

Is there any possibility of leadership from the top? Can we look to General Conference? At present that seems pointless. Can we look to our bishops? That is less hopeless, but it seems that as a group they are not in fact the leaders of the church. My judgment is that, as also in the political sphere, we are wise to give up hope for being guided toward salvation by the official leadership. Perhaps a miracle comparable to what happened in the Roman Catholic Church at Vatican II will happen in the United Methodist Church! For this we can pray, but I see no way to work for it.

There would be much more possibility of breakthroughs into an authentic Wesleyan "economy of salvation" for our time in jurisdictional and annual conferences. This would require some liberation from a General Conference intent on silencing the Spirit. There seemed some hope that North American Methodists could have the same possibility of self-government as the central conferences elsewhere. Still, despite years of serious study and reflection and a promising proposal by a committee mandated by the previous General Conference, the discussion was ultimately blocked. In this context it is difficult to be hopeful that leadership in reflection about, and implementation of, the economy of salvation can be promoted institutionally in the United Methodist Church. With great sadness I feel forced to say that in this time of the greatest crisis in history, I cannot look to the church I love for guidance or help.

However, just as the Wesleyan movement arose in the Church of England without the support of the institutional church, so a movement that genuinely seeks to understand the economy of salvation for our day and to live it out might arise among Wesleyans and might even transform the denomination. That is a lot to hope for, but in a time of desperate danger, we must dare to hope for improbable changes.

5

"Go Tell Pharaoh," or,
Why Empires Prefer a Nameless God

At a portentous moment in the story of the exodus, Pharaoh says to Moses, "Who is the LORD, that I should heed him and let Israel go? I do not know the LORD, and I will not let Israel go" (Exod 5:2). From this point on, the drama of exodus turns on God's promise (or perhaps we should say threat) that "you shall know that I am the LORD" (7:17; 8:22; 9:30). Indeed, the fulfillment of this promise/threat quickly becomes the central subject of the rest of the Bible, which tells how one day not only Pharaoh and the sons and daughters of Israel but all creation shall know "that the LORD is God" (Deut 7:9; Josh 4:24; 1 Sam 17:46; 1 Kgs 8:60; Ps 100:3; Ezek 13:9).

The remarkable character of Moses' exchange with Pharaoh is blunted for us in some degree by the (honorable) conventions of biblical translators. For we must remember that what our English Bibles translate as LORD is in Hebrew a proper name, God's proper name. When Pharaoh scoffs, "I do not know the LORD," his expostulation is identical in force to that of, say, a CEO who has just been informed that a stranger in the outer office, identified only by name, wants him to hand over the corporate assets. Pharaoh's reaction is predictable; the story's outcome is not. What came into being was a people who knew its existence to be tied up with this God's name and the practice of taking it seriously (cf. Exod 20:7).

Over time, the people of Israel came to treat God's proper name with such respect that they ceased to pronounce it altogether, except on the holiest occasions. When the Hebrew Bible was translated into Greek, the

Holy Name was rendered by the common noun *kyrios*, meaning "Lord," and this practice has been followed by most translators of the Bible down to the present day. Still today Jews do not pronounce God's Holy Name, preferring to use some circumlocution such as "The Holy One, Blessed be He," or even more simply *HaShem*, which means "The Name." Yet Israel has never doubted that the One who delivered it from Egypt was not a nameless numinous "X," but the particular One revealed by name to Moses.

Now, it is just at this point that the ancient claim of Jewish faith runs smack into a serious contemporary objection. It is all well and good, so the objection goes, for ancient Israel to have believed that God revealed God's name to it and chose it uniquely to be God's people. This belief, perhaps necessary in its day for the rise of monotheism, has outlived its usefulness and legitimacy. Today it is necessary for the Jewish faith, for the Christian faith, indeed, for all faiths to embark upon a radical paradigm shift: "We need today more than ever a world faith which will provide an effective basis for human solidarity in a shrinking world. For unless we seek to harmonize the religions how shall we ever find that common 'ethos,' that universally accepted system of spiritual values and moral principles which we need in order to overcome our confusion, to end the war of ideologies and give international law and morality a sound foundation?"[1]

Recently this charge has been taken up with great seriousness in an anthology called *The Myth of Christian Uniqueness: Toward a Pluralist Theology of Religions*.[2] While the authors are not of one mind about what a "pluralist theology of religions" would look like, they stress the ineffability of the transcendent referent of religion and hold that differing religions point more or less adequately toward a Reality that is absolutely indescribable. The "transcendent Center . . . remains always beyond and greater than apprehensions of it or even the sum total of such apprehensions." Behind and beyond Israel's LORD God, the Muslims' Allah, the Hindus' Brahman, there lies an ineffable reality that itself never appears except in these scheme-specific manifestations.[3] One author quotes with appreciation a verse from Hindu scripture: "Thou art formless. Thy only form is our knowledge of Thee." For this author, it follows that there can be no such thing as idolatry in the pejorative sense, since all concepts of God are "idols," that is, human constructs. What is to be condemned is the identification of the image with

1. Visser 't Hooft, *No Other Name*, 86.
2. Hick and Knitter, *The Myth of Christian Uniqueness*.
3. DiNoia, "Pluralist Theology of Religions," 129.

the Reality it represents. As one author states, "For Christians to think that Christianity is true, or final, or salvific, is a form of idolatry."[4]

Now, here indeed we are faced with a basic alternative. On the one hand, we have the faith of Israel, which attests to a God who has been revealed by name, who refuses to share glory with any other. On the other hand, we have the appeal to recognize that, strictly speaking, God has no name at all, that God is the ineffable mystery who transcends all the many names for God and to whom all the different religions give access. This alternative is especially momentous for Christians, for it poses once again the ancient question of how Christian faith is or is not related to the jealous God, the LORD God of Israel.

As one who has taught in a seminary for several years, I am well aware that the pluralist proposal is attractive to many people today, including many persons who are deeply concerned about Christian faith. And yet I am convinced that the promise of the pluralist option—namely, that it presents a truer understanding of God that will help humankind transcend its differences—is a dead end, a false promise.

To begin, we should not imagine that the pluralist proposal is something dramatically new in the religious history of humankind. On the contrary, the idea that the divine is utterly transcendent, is strictly nameless and ineffable, is one of the oldest theological views on record. This view was, in fact, well known to Israel's neighbors, the ancient Egyptians. A hymn from an ancient Egyptian papyrus goes as follows: "The One and only, who hides himself from men and gods. No one knows his being. He is higher than the heaven and deeper than the netherworld. No god knows his true appearance. . . . He is too mysterious, one cannot reveal his glory, he is too great to search out, and too powerful to be known."[5] The nameless, ineffable God, then, is not a newcomer to the religious scene. He was, perhaps, precisely the God whom Pharaoh presupposed when he spoke derisively to Moses, "Who is the LORD, that I should heed him and let Israel go?"

The advocates of a pluralist theology of religions, of course, are well aware that the idea of Ultimate Reality as ineffable mystery is not new. In fact, they point to its ubiquity and antiquity as evidence of its deep roots in human experience and as grounds for its acceptance today. Here I think we come to a key question: the nameless, ineffable God has deep roots in human experience. But what experience is this? Or to put it another way, on

4. Smith, "Idolatry," 56.
5. Quoted in Gerlitz, "Name/Namengebung I," 746.

whose behalf does the nameless, ineffable God reign? In fairness, we must say that the human spirit has been drawn to speak this way of God for many reasons, including awe and humility before the mystery of life. Yet we may at least ask whether the cult of the ineffable God owes some of its appeal to its political utility, especially for empires, which by their nature seek to unite many peoples, cultures, and religions under a single earthly authority. In the famous words of Edward Gibbon, in the age of the Caesars all modes of worship were "considered by the people equally true, by the philosophers equally false, and by the magistrates equally useful."[6]

We have already seen that ancient Egypt knew of the cult of the ineffable God. Yet it was Alexander the Great who, by conquering the whole eastern Mediterranean in a few short years, created the social and political conditions in which the cult of the nameless, ineffable God attained prominence in the Western world. According to New Testament scholar James Dunn, the theology that underlay the policy of Alexander the Great and his Greek and Latin successors regarded the different religions as in the end only manifestations of the same deities.[7] This theology allowed the victors to incorporate defeated nations by absorbing the local religions into the larger syncretistic whole of the empire. So, for example, the Greek God Zeus and Roman God Jupiter were regarded as one and the same; at Bath in England, we find a statue to Minerva-Sulis, Minerva being the Roman goddess and Sulis the local equivalent. In the great hymns to the Egyptian goddess Isis, she was addressed as "Thou of countless names," because she was identified with so many different religions.

Gradually, among the learned, the religious attitude took hold that the different religions were in fact only manifestations of the one deity or, in the words of a treatise falsely attributed to Aristotle, "God being one yet has many names."[8] This view, philosophically buttressed by the successive waves of Platonic revival that emphasized, in addition to God's unity, his utter transcendence and ineffability, became in fact the reigning civic religion of the ancient imperial world. We should not be too surprised, then, to learn that the Emperor Alexander Severus had in his private chapel not only the statues of the deified emperors but also those of the miracle worker Apollonius of Tyana, of Christ, of Abraham, and of Orpheus.[9]

6. Gibbon, *History*, 18.
7. Dunn, *Partings of the Ways*, 20.
8. Grant, *Gods*, 77.
9. Visser 't Hooft, *No Other Name*, 15.

Of course, the success of the imperial theology depended in part on the willingness of the subjugated to identify their own deities with other gods. In general, this was not much of an obstacle, for many ancient people were eager to keep their religious portfolios in balance. If eternal reality is ultimately unknowable, it is best to take advantage of emerging opportunities to participate as fully as possible in the life of the gods.[10] In the case of the Jews, however, the policy did not work. When Antiochus Epiphanes, one of Alexander's regional successors, tried to set up a cult of Zeus in the Temple of Jerusalem, he was simply following the logic of imperial theology. In his view the LORD God was simply the local manifestation of Zeus (2 Macc 6:1–2). The Jews did not see it that way, and the incident set off the Maccabean revolt and the eventual repurification of the temple which is celebrated today in the festival of Chanukah. Even such thoroughly Hellenized men as the Jew Philo and the Christian Origen (both residents, we may note, of the imperial city Alexandria in Egypt) refused to identify the God who spoke to Moses with any other god or deity known to the ancient world. When the emperor Caligula decreed that his image should be venerated in the temple in Jerusalem, Philo risked his life by joining a delegation sent to the emperor in protest. Origen declared that Christians would rather die than call God "Zeus" and was imprisoned and tortured for his refusal to burn incense to Caesar.

In light of incidents such as these, we can understand, I think, the threat that the God of exodus posed to the ancient God of imperial religion. Moreover, we can understand the widespread belief among cultured Hellenists in the Graeco-Roman world that Jews (and later Christians) were atheists—not because they were monotheists but because they were exclusive monotheists.[11] For if different religions are simply different local manifestations of the same deities, and if furthermore all these are simply manifestations of the one supreme being who is nameless and ineffable, then to speak of a God who has revealed himself by name in the exodus is in fact to abandon the proper worship of God altogether.

Today, the authors of *The Myth of Christian Uniqueness* have renewed the call to worship the nameless, ineffable One who is manifest through the variety of religions. While they do not charge Christians and Jews with being atheists, they do imply, as we saw earlier, that "for Christians to think

---

10. Ibid., 16.

11. Dunn, *Partings of the Ways*, 20.

that Christianity is true, or final, or salvific, is a form of idolatry."[12] Yet here again, I think, we do well to ask whether there may not be a hidden, imperial spirit that animates this proposal, much against the good intentions of the authors themselves. A telling clue in this respect is found in the book's preface, in which coeditor Paul Knitter writes, "We wanted to gather theologians who were exploring the possibilities of a *pluralist* position—a move away from insistence on the superiority or finality of Christ and Christianity toward a recognition of the independent validity of other ways. Such a move came to be described by participants in our project as the crossing of a theological Rubicon."[13] The image is ironic, of course, for Julius Caesar's crossing of that same river in 49 BCE was "a forceful attempt to encompass the 'other' within his own framework."[14]

Is there in fact a modern "empire" today, similar in its sheer power and territorial ambitions to the ancient empires of Egypt, of Alexander, of the Roman Caesars? The answer, I think, is yes. Today the counterpart to the ancient empires is the power of the marketplace and the penetration of market rationality into ever new domains of life. In its attempt to subordinate the Holy One of Israel to the nameless ineffable One, to the nameless God with many names, the pluralist theology of religion unwittingly provides a spiritual rationale for the unlimited dominance of the marketplace, for the commodification of all things, including religion and, indeed, human life itself.

From time immemorial, humans have engaged in market exchange. The market operates by creating a place where persons can freely produce and exchange commodities according to the laws of supply and demand without interference from outside forces. What distinguishes the modern world is not the existence of markets but the increasingly large place that markets and market logic have taken in Western society. In exchange for this larger space, the market has delivered an unprecedented growth in wealth and material standards of living for many tens of millions of people. Yet the growth of the market has not been without costs. Throughout the eighteenth and nineteenth centuries, the growth of the market was accompanied by the gradual dissolution of other modes of organizing society based on tradition, kinship, religion, and government. From the point of view of the market, these older forms of relation were inefficient, that is,

12. Smith, "Idolatry," 59.
13. Hick and Knitter, *Myth of Christian Uniqueness*, viii.
14. D'Costa, *Christian Uniqueness*, ix.

they created obstacles to the free exchange of goods and the accumulation of wealth. The growth of the market therefore demanded that these relationships be gradually dissolved and reshaped in a more rational way, one that serves and responds to the demands of the marketplace.

Over time, the growth of the liberal market society has helped shape a new kind of person, a new "I." Since the economic world is one of constant innovation and flux, the new individuated person is supposed to be free of constraints, unrestricted in his or her inward life by any bonds to external authority. Charles Taylor remarks that the new self is constructed as a rational individual who chooses "not to identify with any of the tendencies he finds in himself, which can only be the deposits of tradition and authority, but to be ready to break and remake these habitual responses according to his own goals." The result is the construction of the "I" as a pure unencumbered self, existing independent of relationships and ready to act for the sake of greater material reward.[15]

In light of this, we should not be too surprised by the re-emergence of the proposal for religious pluralism, which, if I am right, has long been the native theology of empire. I do not think that the advocates of a pluralist theology of religions wish to underwrite the imperial logic of the marketplace. Indeed, I think their desire is to do exactly the opposite. Nevertheless, if their proposal proves widely popular, I think it will be because it serves so well to provide an account of religion that mirrors the logic of the marketplace and thus also gives the market a theological justification.

Consider three ways in which the pluralist theology of religions reflects and thereby underwrites the logic of the marketplace. In the first place, the pluralist theology of religion transforms the different religions, each with its own unique theologies, social formations, and claims to truth, into essentially interchangeable paths or vehicles to the same end. In effect, the pluralist theology turns the religions into a kind of spiritual commodity, which may differ from one another for the purposes of attracting adherents (i.e., advertising) but which are in substance all offering exactly the same product. Second, the pluralist theology teaches that the end or goal of all the various religions is not identical with any of the religions but remains an ineffable, unknown X that transcends them all, a locus of pure numinous power and salvation. Here the analogy to the imperial market is especially eerie; for the market too spins around a center that is itself utterly without form, namely, pure wealth as power. What drives the market is not

15. Taylor, "Inwardness and the Culture of Modernity," 613.

any particular form of wealth but wealth as such, which may temporarily reside in dollars, yen, stock, or real estate, but which in itself transcends them all. Finally, the pluralist theology of religions suggests that since no religion is superior to any other, all persons are free to choose the image of God that he or she finds most congenial. As Lesslie Newbigin has pointed out, this final implication surreptitiously elevates the self into a position of command and corresponds "to the ethos of the consumer society where the choice of the customer is free and sovereign."[16]

Of course, I do not know whether the pluralist proposal will take hold in the coming decades and whether it will in fact come to provide something like the plausibility structure of the new global marketplace. Yet I am certain of at least two things. Like all empires, the imperial market will continue to exact frightening costs from the human community. The market, of course, promises to make the consumer king and encourages us to think that we are in charge. The market charges a high price in return, namely, the increasing commodification of human life itself. To take just one example, as genetic knowledge becomes more complete and available to consumers through law, prospective parents will be pressured to screen their pregnancies in order to screen out inefficiencies such as mental retardation and other genetic disorders. The other thing I am certain of is this: the ineffable God of the pluralists will be powerless to deliver humankind from its plight. Increasingly, I believe, people will refuse to be satisfied with the promises of gods who are ineffable, who cannot or will not reveal their name. In the midst of their groaning, people will demand to know from those who presume to speak for God, "Who is it that sent you? What is his name?"

I have already noted that central to biblical faith is God's promise to Israel that Israel, the nations, and all the earth will come to confess that "the LORD is God!" What shall we make of this? Let us begin with this simple observation. For biblical faith, it goes to the very heart of the matter to recognize that although God cannot be circumscribed, God can be identified. To say that God cannot be circumscribed is to say that human beings can never bring God under their control. God is inexhaustible. Here is the element of truth in the position of the pluralist theologians. God cannot be caught by our definitions or domesticated by human thought or feeling. Moreover, the pluralists are correct in saying that any name that we give

16. Newbigin, "Religion for the Marketplace," 146.

to God falls short of God's own reality. Although humans are name-giving animals, they cannot give a name to God.

The Bible makes clear that while God cannot be circumscribed, God can be identified. Note: God is identifiable not because God's namelessness sets us free to give God names according to our own predilections. Rather, God is identifiable because God reveals God's name to us and in doing so casts aside all our self-serving talk of God. This is precisely what God does in his encounter with Moses. Here it is of inestimable significance that God reveals God's name to Moses in the context of the exodus. For biblical faith, the name of God is inseparable from the stories and narratives that delineate God's actions. God's name comes with a specific history. In that history, as we see in the exodus, is the creation of freedom.

Many today think of freedom on the model of consumer choice: to be free is to have many options, regardless of what particular option one might pick. That is not the biblical understanding of freedom. The story of the exodus makes clear that God's name promises and creates freedom with a definite content. In the first place, God creates freedom for those who are threatened by the empires of their day—for those who, in the words of Gustavo Gutiérrez, are "non-persons," those whose lives and deaths are of no official account. In the second place, the freedom that God creates is for life lived in community with others. Long before the exodus, God promised Abraham that in him all the nations of the earth would be blessed. The prophets continually looked forward to the time when this promise will be fulfilled, and when all the nations shall dwell together in peace with God, with one another, and with the natural world.

Both biblical faith and the pluralist theologians affirm the mystery of God. Yet the two positions have very different understandings of God's mystery. For the pluralists, God's mystery means that in the final analysis God remains hidden and ineffable. This is what I have sometimes called the Monty Hall understanding of mystery. God is a mystery in the way that contestants on *Let's Make a Deal* do not know what is behind door number three. In the words of the ancient Egyptian prayer, "No god knows his true appearance. . . . He is too mysterious, one cannot reveal his glory, he is too great to search out, and too powerful to be known."[17] This understanding of mystery is actually a prison beyond which God cannot move. For the pluralists, the one thing God can never do is reveal his name, for to do so would be to expose the mystery.

17. Gerlitz, "Name/Namengebung I," 746.

Biblical faith understands God's mystery in an entirely different way. God is not restricted by the prison of ineffability. God's mystery is not something that God must protect by remaining inaccessible and ineffable. For biblical faith, the mystery of God is that God wants to be known. The mystery of God is that God steps out of the "ineffability" beloved by Greeks and makes Godself addressable, nameable, and vulnerable. The mystery of God is not what we do not know about God but precisely what God shows to us, namely, that God is, in the words of Mary, one who "has brought down the powerful from their thrones, and lifted up the lowly; he has filled the hungry with good things, and sent the rich away empty" (Luke 1:52–53). The mystery of this God is not that he chooses to remain inaccessible but that he freely shares his life with his creatures. No matter how much they may draw upon him, he remains ever inexhaustible and generous.

For biblical faith, the mystery of God is also this: that in coming to know God, in coming to bless God's name, we also come to know ourselves and one another. Notice that if God is ineffable, then ultimately each religion stands on its own as an independent avenue toward God, and indeed, each tradition and each person comes to stand on its own. For if God is ineffable, then the search for God ultimately becomes an individual quest in which each person sets out in pursuit of the image that is most congenial. The mystery of the biblical God is not something that can be discovered by each person on his or her own. On the contrary, the mystery of the biblical God is that we can only come to know and to praise this God in the company of others whom God provides as our companions. To know God, we must be open to one another. Israel's life with God cannot happen apart from the nations, and the nations cannot live with God apart from Israel.

From this it follows, too, that our names, our identities are important. This is not at all clear from the pluralist perspective. For the pluralists, since God is the ineffable X, one cannot even say that the X is personal and relates to us in a personal way. Hence one cannot say whether our own personal identities are of ultimate significance to God. For the Hindu, for example, salvation consists in the dissolution of the self; for pluralists, this is at least as accurate as the biblical teaching that humankind is created in the image and likeness of God.

From the biblical perspective, who we are matters, which is why the Bible takes names so seriously. Have you noticed that the Bible is filled with proper names? A proper name is the very opposite of a commodity. Each name and its history is unique and non-interchangeable. Hence the biblical

God alone, I think, has the power to resist the forces of the contemporary empire, namely the market, which pushes toward the commodification of all things, including human life itself. The Pharaoh regarded Israel as a nameless mass for producing bricks, as units of productive power. In calling them, in hearing their groans, God made them a people, bestowed on them a name, and delivered them from an imperial power that treated them as expendable and interchangeable.

I firmly believe that there is a power that can deliver humankind from its groaning, and that power is in the name of the LORD. Apart from this power, humankind is helpless before the nameless, faceless, impersonal powers of this world. In this name, there is salvation, righteousness, wholeness, and peace. This brings me to a final name, the name of Jesus Christ.

It is extremely important that at several points when the Apostolic Witness wants to get across the incomparable significance of Jesus Christ, it finds it necessary to speak of him in relationship to God's name. All four Gospels, for example, record the fact that when Jesus entered the Holy City riding on an ass, the crowds went before him, singing the messianic psalm, "Blessed is the one who comes in the name of the Lord." Similarly, the Gospel of John records that when Jesus prayed on behalf of the disciples in the High Priestly prayer, he said, "Holy Father, protect them in your name that you have given me, so that they may be one, as we are one" (John 17:11b). Perhaps most famously, the great hymn in Philippians declares that "he humbled himself, and became obedient to the point of death—even death on a cross. Therefore God also highly exalted him and gave him the name that is above every name, so that at the name of Jesus every knee should bend, in heaven and on earth and under the earth, and every tongue should confess that Jesus Christ is Lord, to the glory of God the Father" (2:8–11). In this hymn, the name that the Father gives to Jesus, the name that is above every name, is none other than the holy name signified by the title of Lord. What are we to make of these declarations? Shall we say, as Christians have sometimes said, that these and similar passages intend to suggest that the name of Jesus Christ supersedes and replaces the holy name that God revealed to Moses? Shall we say that the holy name worshiped by the Jewish people has for Christians become a thing of memory only, a reality of the past? I do not think so.

Rather, I think these and similar passages are nudging us toward the recognition that the whole life of Jesus Christ is God's own exegesis, in the medium of humanity, of the content of the divine name.[18] When John declares that "the Word was with God, and the Word was God," and "the Word became flesh and dwelt among us," can he be pointing to anything other than that unique Word which is God's name (John 1:14a)?

If God is the nameless, ineffable X that stands equidistant behind and above all the world's spiritual questing and confusion, then the empires of this world are safe. They may struggle for supremacy with one another, but they need not fear a fundamental challenge from beyond. A nameless God is infinitely malleable, readily adaptable to the needs of the ruler and hence ultimately unreliable from the perspective of those who are enslaved and perishing. If God is not nameless, if God is the One whose name was disclosed to Moses at the burning bush, then the empires of this world are threatened at their very foundations. For the One who declares, "You shall know that I am the LORD!" is a God who refuses to be turned into a commodity by the powerful and who refuses to countenance the commodification of God's creatures. Blessed be the name of the Lord.

Bibliography

D'Costa, Gavin, ed. *Christian Uniqueness Reconsidered: The Myth of a Pluralistic Theology of Religions.* Maryknoll, NY: Orbis, 1990.

DiNoia, J. A. "Pluralist Theology of Religions: Pluralistic or Non-Pluralistic?" In *Christian Uniqueness Reconsidered: The Myth of a Pluralistic Theology of Religions*, edited by Gavin D'Costa, . Maryknoll, NY: Orbis, 1990.

Dunn, James D. G. *The Partings of the Ways: Between Christianity and Judaism and Their Significance for the Character of Christianity.* Philadelphia: Trinity, 1991.

Gerlitz, Peter. "Name/Namengebung I." In *Theologische Realenzyklopädie*, edited by Gerhard Müller, 23:743–47. Berlin: de Gruyter, 1994.

Gibbon, Edward. *History of the Decline and Fall of the Roman Empire.* Vol. 1. London: Jones, 1826.

Grant, Robert M. *Gods and the One God.* Philadelphia: Westminster, 1986.

Hick, John, and Paul F. Knitter, eds. *The Myth of Christian Uniqueness: Toward a Pluralistic Theology of Religions.* Maryknoll, NY: Orbis, 1987.

Newbigin, Lesslie. "Religion for the Marketplace." In *Christian Uniqueness Reconsidered: The Myth of a Pluralistic Theology of Religions*, edited by Gavin D'Costa, 135–48. Maryknoll, NY: Orbis, 1990.

Smith, Wilfred Cantwell. "Idolatry: In Comparative Perspective." In *The Myth of Christian Uniqueness: Toward a Pluralistic Theology of Religions*, edited by John Hick and Paul F. Knitter, 53–68. Maryknoll, NY: Orbis, 1987.

Soulen, Kendall. *The Divine Name(s) and the Holy Trinity.* Vol. 1, *Discerning the Voices.* Louisville: Westminster John Knox, 2011.

18. I elaborate this idea in *The Divine Name(s)*, 191–255.

Taylor, Charles. "Inwardness and the Culture of Modernity." In *Zwischenbetrachtungen: Im Prozeß der Aufklärung*, edited by Axel Honneth et al., 601–23. Frankfurt: Suhrkamp, 1989.

Visser 't Hooft, W. A. *No Other Name: The Choice between Syncretism and Christian Universalism*. Philadelphia: Westminster, 1963.

6

M. Douglas Meeks: Process Theologian

MARJORIE HEWITT SUCHOCKI

The purpose of this essay may seem strange: I will argue that implicit within the work of Doug Meeks are assumptions that are grounded in process philosophy, so that to his titles—biblical theologian, liberation theologian, and theology of hope theologian—he should add a fourth: M. Douglas Meeks, Process Theologian. I proceed by comments on his work in *God the Economist*, followed by a description of process philosophy. Drawing out some of the theological implications of process philosophy as developed by process theologians, I then seek to show how Meeks, working explicitly with biblical and theological concepts, is also working implicitly with process concepts—enough to justify naming him a process theologian.

In *God the Economist*, Meeks accomplishes an astonishing feat in the history of theology by turning the long-dominant notion of omnipotence on its head. The primary notion of God within the Western Christian tradition has been that of omnipotence. Twice within the very brief and very early Apostles' Creed there is a reference to God's omnipotence, with nary a mention of the other two assigned characteristics of deity: omniscience and omnipresence. The creed was reflective of the sensitivities of its age that God, to be God, must assuredly be all-powerful. In this, Greek philosophy rather than biblical notions most strongly shaped the emerging Christian doctrine of God, and God's power then became the interpretive lens through which God's knowledge and God's presence were understood. Omniscience understood through omnipotence led to various theories of predestination (for how could so little a thing as human freedom shape the activities of an omnipotent deity?), and divine presence was most often understood through the analogy of a king's power present throughout his realm.

Yet in *God the Economist*, Meeks very intentionally challenges omnipotence and its corollary, domination, as defining characteristics of God. In doing so, Meeks works primarily through biblical texts and traditional doctrines of the Trinity. His work finds its place within liberation theology, both in its North American forms and in their European counterparts, notably through Jürgen Moltmann's theology of hope. In all forms of these theologies, the notion of God as omnipotent is so counter to the experience of oppression that the power of God must itself be transformed from a power over to a power with. Liberation theologians usually repudiate God as a dominating power, embracing instead God's empowering power that enables humans to resist dominating oppressions. So too, Meeks finds that the Bible, once one ceases to read it through the lens of Greek philosophy, is a loud cry for liberation from economies of oppression to the renewing work of the economy of God. Omnipotence crumbles; in its place omnipresence becomes the defining mark of deity, grounding the new understanding of God's power in an empowering power of presence.

In Meeks's brilliant analysis of biblical texts, God is economist in the biblical sense of the word, establishing and enabling communities as inclusive households, ever vigilant for the physical well-being of all inhabitants. Meeks thoroughly repudiates a God of coercive, dominating power. In its place, God is an economist, providing life-giving structures for society. The motif of the "stranger within your gates" extends such hospitality to those outside the household. Justice as well-being cannot be confined; to limit justice anywhere is to challenge justice everywhere.

When "power" is so radically restructured in and through omnipresence, implications follow for the other member of the "omni" triad, omniscience. When we begin with omnipresence as the basis of God's power and knowledge, then we find that the "omni" usually associated with these terms in reference to God becomes a term connoting "all-relational" instead of its usual function of ultimacy.

As a process theologian, I am interested in the implicit as well as explicit restructuring of omnipotence, omniscience, and omnipresence that occurs through Meeks's work, finding process concepts rampant. He provides biblical and trinitarian arguments; but if we seek the philosophical grounding of his conceptual structure, we must turn to process thought.

Process, almost alone among philosophical alternatives, strengthens notions of God as engendering liberating power in society, primarily because God works through a power of presence. In order to explore these issues in relation to Meeks's work, it is necessary to provide a brief overview of process philosophy.

Process Philosophy in Brief

Process philosophy provides a model for understanding existence within a radically relational world. Throughout Christian history, theologians have utilized philosophical models of reality in their explication of Christian faith. Plato, Aristotle, and Plotinus were woven into Christian faith for much of Christian history, supplemented with models drawn from nominalism in the late Middle Ages, followed by the Enlightenment philosophers. Phenomenology, existentialisms, and linguistic philosophies played roles in twentieth-century philosophy. With few exceptions, "substance" was the basic philosophical category, with substance being that which needs nothing other than itself in order to exist. In a world of relativity physics, this becomes a category mistake: nothing exists apart from relation to that which is other to itself.

Henri Bergson in the nineteenth century and Samuel Alexander in the early twentieth began the process of reforming the philosophical understanding of reality, moving away from the classical notion of substance toward views of constant creativity. Emergence took the place of substance. Alfred North Whitehead, likewise, asked questions about reality that pushed toward answers of emergence, creativity, dynamism, and relationality. His *Process and Reality* was published in 1929; it represents his answer to questions raised by relativity physics: what must the fundamental nature of reality be, if at its most elemental level it occurs in droplets of relationality? Underlying our everyday experience of selves and tables and chairs and all that we construe as our "world," there is a radical indeterminacy of constant becoming, and this becoming is radically relational. Whitehead coined the term "actual occasion" (or, when the notion of God is included, "actual entity") to refer to each droplet of becoming. Most of *Process and Reality* is an exploration of what might—or must—be the case for these occasions to occur at all.

Because Whitehead was discussing reality at a level never before addressed in philosophy, he invented a vocabulary to describe what had not been described before. On the one hand, his new vocabulary had the advantage of shedding suppositions built into all our philosophical concepts, thus allowing a keener analysis. Yet on the other, precisely because the language was new, Whitehead's philosophy defied easy access. His Gifford Lectures, which became *Process and Reality*, famously began with a rather large audience, but as the five lectures progressed, the audience became smaller and smaller—a mere five persons attended the final lecture. Despite the challenge of summarizing so complex a system, I do so because it provides an astonishing basis for understanding the theological concept of God's omnipresence and therefore allows further explication of how we might interpret God's power and wisdom as grounded in God's presence.

Imagine, then, this "droplet of experience," this "actual occasion," not before all existence but in the midst of existence, coming into existence in response to its particular past and in light of its possible future. Because the actual occasion presupposes a past of many actual occasions and a future of occasions that must take account of what this actual occasion has become, the oddity occurs that we must build its description even while presupposing its description. No wonder that Whitehead needed a new vocabulary to describe so relational a basis to all existence! So, then, imagine that each finished actual occasion demands an accounting of itself and that our now imagined droplet of experience, our actual occasion, emerges in response to these demands.

Notice at once that any emerging occasion out of an entire past's demands is faced with an overwhelming problem of selection from forced alternatives. Each occasion in the past demands its own repetition in the present; its own conclusion contains a strong appetition for some form of continuance in the emerging entity. This is the inescapable relationality of existence. The very emergence of the becoming occasion is predicated upon its responsive feelings of its past.

Whitehead insisted on the term "feelings," even though he was not discussing reality at the level of sentient beings. Indeed, he used his own term, "prehension," as a synonym for "feelings." By these words—feelings or prehensions—he indicated a kind of transfer of energy from one occasion that impels the becoming of another. From the point of view of the transmitting occasion, these feelings are an appetition for its future; from the point of view of the emerging occasion, these feelings are its initial formation that call it into being as it takes into its emergent self the appetitive feelings of the other. Relation is constitutive of reality.

If there were simply one occasion in the past calling forth a new becoming in a new present, then reality would simply be an everlasting continuance of itself with neither variation nor novelty. But the past is incomprehensively vast, which leads to the problem mentioned above of selectivity. Out of a multitude of feelings of a multitude of entities, each of which demands its own repetition, how is anything to become at all? Why does not the whole process break down into absolute chaos? How is there order? This very problem is why Whitehead is forced to include a notion of God in his system. He resisted recourse to God. He adamantly refused a sort of Molierian solution of the knight dressed in shining armor, arriving on stage at the last minute, mounted on a great white horse, unsnarling all the knots left over from the drama. If Whitehead had to use a notion of God to introduce order and novelty in the midst of chaos, then Whitehead thought he could only do so responsibly if the notion of God he developed was consistent with the whole of his analysis. God would not be an exception to the metaphysical principles laid down by the system as a whole but would in fact be their chief exemplification.

And so, apart from immediate recourse to Part V of *Process and Reality*, think of it this way. Each actual occasion will be described in terms of its emergence through physical feelings of everything in its past—including now its feelings of God's feelings for its possible future. Each actual occasion will then be analyzed as proceeding through a process of comparing its various feelings, negating some, adapting others, toward a vision of what it might become. This vision can be an inchoate sense of what might yet be, given what has been received. Yet in some basic sense it is a mental pole, balancing the physical pole of its beginnings. The process of becoming moves from a physical pole derived from its past and from God, through a process of comparisons, evaluations, and judgments that ultimately results in a satisfaction of the whole process. This satisfaction is Janus-faced. On the one hand, it is completion, looking back on itself. It has finished its task; it has become. On the other hand, it is appetition. Given that it has become, a new future can emerge in which its own subjectivity will be objectively included. Just as it has taken the past into itself, even so its immediate successors will take its own feelings into their becoming selves.

Notice the interplay of subjectivity and objectivity that occurs in the whole process. Subjectivity always refers to the becomingness of the present. Everything that becomes, every actual occasion, is its own subject, determining itself out of its past and its possibilities. Yet once it is finished,

its subjectivity is over. It now becomes data for a new subject; it is objecti-
fied by the becoming future. Relative to its own subjectivity, the entity is
free to become as it will within its parameters. Still its freedom dies with
itself; it is object relative to others. This facet of the process model leads to
interesting permutations when taken to the level of our everyday world of
being a self amidst others, where intensity of value calls on each to reckon
with the subjectivity, not the objectivity, of all becoming others. Further
exploration at this point would deflect us too much from the task at hand,
which is to explore the process basis for insisting upon God's omnipresence
as fundamental to all existence.

The point of these last two paragraphs is that each finite actual occasion begins with the physical pole and concludes in satisfaction with the
mental pole. There is an inexorable procession from feelings of otherness
to the satisfaction of one's own becoming through the mental pole. The
problem of suggesting that God is required to provide a basis for novelty
and order instead of random chaos and at the same time to keep the understanding of God within the metaphysical principles of the actual entity
is that if God also progresses from physical pole to the mental pole, then
God as well as everything else requires a basis for its future beyond the
resources of the past alone. We have infinite regress, not resolution. So
Whitehead played with this innovative notion: what if God, as an actual
entity, exhibits all the metaphysical qualities of the actual occasion but in
reverse order? What if God begins everlastingly in the mental pole and progresses through ever incorporating the world into the divine self through
the physical pole? Would this solve the problem of infinite regress and at
the same time provide a means for introducing novelty and order into the
world—indeed, the universe?

Whitehead begins the arduous process of reconfiguring the notion of
God in a universe like ours, where radical relationality at the most fundamental level produces a universe of stars and nebulae, comets and asteroids,
planets and people and all manner of growing things in various combinations of order and chaos, stability and novelty. The mental pole is a vision
of what might be, the home of possibilities. Suppose that God everlastingly
"begins" in a mental pole, including the satisfaction that adheres to each
mental pole. If God is everlasting, then God's mental pole, before and with
all times, must be an infinite vision of all possibilities whatsoever, in infinite
varieties of combinations, like a constantly moving panorama of ever-shift-
ing combinations of possibilities but always exhibiting harmony: beauty,

order, zest, adventure, peace. An essential dynamism within satisfaction is necessary if God everlastingly "begins" in the mental pole. Nor would this be a beginning in the temporal sense; to the contrary, for metaphysical reasons, it would have to be eternal and intensely dynamic.

What, then, of God's physical pole? Whitehead defines this pole as the feeling of others. Through these feelings, these "prehensions," an entity takes that which is other into the becoming self. If God exemplifies the metaphysics, then God everlastingly feels every actual entity upon its completion, taking the feeling of that entity into Godself.

The physical pole is integrated into the mental through a process of comparisons and judgments, into the vision of what might be, which then yields a satisfaction that looks beyond itself toward possible futures in which it is included. Beginning rather than ending with the mental pole, God's integration of the world within the divine self would be into a vision that is primordial, everlastingly actualizing it in infinite permutations of harmony. Because of the reversal of the polar structure, God is always complete and always in the process of completion. God's satisfaction, likewise, undergirds the everlasting integration of all things within God and yields ever new possibilities for the becoming world.

Return, now, to the becoming occasion in the world. This emergent occasion must feel every entity in its relative past—but God is in that relative past as an everlasting satisfaction everlastingly feeling new possibilities for the world in every standpoint. Bear in mind that God has already felt every element in the becoming occasion's past—God, and only God, knows everything the becoming entity has to deal with, and God has integrated all entities in that past within God, judging and transforming the past in accordance with the divine satisfaction. Emerging from this satisfaction are appetitive feelings for what possibilities are now relevant to the world, together with a valuation of those possibilities in terms of what can lead to the most complexity, the most intensity, the most good. Thus the possibilities God feels for the emergent entity are relevant to that past but provide possibilities for how that past might yield a novel future in the emergent entity. Thus the entity's feelings of God along with its past is a feeling of ways that it might deal creatively with its welter of influences. So Whitehead calls this feeling from God an "initial aim," a guiding influence in light of the past. God becomes the source of novelty that is (to adopt a phrase made popular in womanist theology) "a way out of no way."

What the emerging occasion does with this initial aim from God is up to the occasion itself. It is a guiding influence, not a controlling influence. Its power is its relevance to the situation. Yet since this aim stems from God's own feeling of possibilities relative to the emerging world, depending upon the complexity of the emerging entity's location, the aim from God can be like a cluster of possible ways to deal with the past. Thus the emergent occasion can feel more than one compatible alternative within the guidance received from God. An irreducible freedom exists within every entity to become itself within relevant alternatives. The occasion is finally responsible for what it does with its alternatives. Thus God's power within this system is a persuasive power, not coercive power, and a guiding rather than a controlling power. It is ultimately a power based upon relational presence.

In a radically relational universe, God's omnipresence is the basis of God's power and God's knowledge. God continuously receives the newly completed entities of the world within Godself, there to do with the world as God will in the process of judging that world. God knows the world "feelingly," by feeling the world as it felt itself. As God integrates these feelings within the depths of the divine nature, the world is transformed within God according to God's vision. This, of course, becomes a basis for a process eschatology. God is the resurrection of the world, the judgment of the world, and the transformer of the world—in theological parlance, God is redeemer and perfecter of the world. Yet it also forms the basis of God's knowledge. In most of the Christian tradition, omniscience was an extension of omnipotence and as such it fell prey to conundrums such as requiring God to know things that had not yet happened as if they had happened. The temporal universe lost its temporality within the knowledge of God, who always saw the world as a completed whole. Finite freedom was either illusory or a mystery over against the ultimacy of God's power and God's knowledge.

When one starts with omnipresence instead of omnipotence, the whole equation shifts. Because of divine presence, God knows the world as it has known itself in its infinite variety of standpoints. God knows the past as past relative to the becoming world in all its standpoints. God knows what possibilities are currently relevant to the becoming world. God knows what probable trajectories could take place, given the choices taking place in the becoming world. God's knowledge is perfect because God knows reality as it was, as it is, and as it can be from an infinite variety of perspectives. Because God is present to reality as it is, God knows reality as it is; and such knowledge is perfect.

The power of God's presence is, as discussed above, persuasive. Yet it is also enabling: God offers the world "a way out of no way," a possibility that is at the same time a power to become that possibility. Apart from the aim of God, there is only chaos; with the aim of God, chaos becomes the cradle for creative evolution—not simply once, in a long-ago past, but continuously.

The theological category most apt to describe the omnipresence, omnipotence, and omniscience of God in process thought is "grace." The "omni" in the words, of course, has shifted in meaning from "ultimacy" to "all-relational." Grace does not depend upon merit. God is not present to us because we deserve it. God is present to us because it is in the nature of God to be present to us and in the character of God to be present to us as an ever-present help in time of trouble and, indeed, in all times.

Theologically considered, God's grace goes before us; it is "prevenient." Grace calls us to conformity to God and enables that conformity—as is so, in process thought, with the initial aim. Theologically considered, God's grace is justifying or pardoning. The connotation is that grace is cleansing, a washing away of that which hinders us and a making of all things new. The basis of this justifying work is God's taking of our whole selves, including our sin, into Godself, along with its consequence of death. Within God, God overturns death into judgment and resurrection, from which new possibilities for finite life constantly stream.

Philosophically, God continuously takes finite existence, including its consequences, into Godself for the sake of judgment and transformation that can yield new possibilities for renewed life in the world. Theologically considered, God's grace is perfecting, sanctifying. Philosophically, God's aims are toward moving beyond debilitating pasts into new forms of intensity and complexity, toward the end of greater communities of well-being. "Grace" is a theological term expressing dynamics that are essential to process philosophy.

Process and *God the Economist*

This excursion into process philosophy and theology brings us back again to the issues so profoundly developed by Doug Meeks in *God the Economist*. Meeks uses biblical exegesis and the implications of God as triune to make his powerful argument for justice in communities of well-being. Undergirding contemporary economic theories and practices are models of domination that gain wealth for the few at the expense of the welfare of the many. Models of domination, in their turn, reflect ideals embedded within the very notion of omnipotence as the ultimate symbol of supreme power. Meeks breaks the model of omnipotence, drawing instead from liberating implications found in biblical and Christian theologies of a very different kind of power: a power for communal well-being.

Meeks is not doing philosophical theology. Every theology, biblical or otherwise, has within it implicit assumptions about the nature of reality, and I am suggesting that the entirety of *God the Economist* rests upon assumptions developed explicitly within process philosophy and its counterpart, process theology. The most obvious of these assumptions, of course, is the redefinition of divine power. For Meeks, as for process, divine power is relational: it is a calling and enabling power. Further, it is a power that gives of itself. While Meeks develops this in and through biblical witness, process develops it through its analysis of the fundamental nature of existence. The initial aim is not only calling and enabling but stems from God's own being; it is a self-sharing aim. Neither in Meeks nor in process thought is God's self-sharing coercive.

In *God the Economist*, God's creative and empowering call is always toward communal well-being. Meeks is at pains to develop this in terms of the entirety of human life—our physical needs, our need for work, our relation to property, our relation to one another in communities seeking the welfare of all. Philosophically, God's aim is always communal in orientation. God aims at intensity of experience, and such intensity depends upon increasing capacities for reciprocal well-being. Aims are always given to individual actual occasions in light of the widest possible good in ever-wider communities of well-being. Aims are social, never individualistic. How could they be, given that all reality is relational through and through? Thus process philosophy undergirds Meeks's redevelopment of economics and community.

It is fairly simple to point out how the relational theology emerging from process philosophy underlies the work Meeks develops from biblical exegesis. Yet he also relies, throughout his work, on a particular notion of the economic trinity. For Meeks, as for the tradition, the economic trinity is the extra-trinitarian expression of the inner-trinitarian life of God. Process philosophy is not trinitarian in the usual Christian sense of the term. Joseph Bracken is perhaps an exception here, developing out of process metaphysics a communal notion of God as trinity. While I also have a communal notion of God, neither my work nor Bracken's is traditionally trinitarian, whereas Meeks's is. Yet I think even here, if we look at Meeks's description of God as triune, there are foundational overtones in process philosophy. I refer specifically to the qualities Meeks attaches to God as creator, redeemer, and perfecter, traditionally called Father, Son, and Spirit. While the quality of suffering is usually attributed to God incarnate as Son, Meeks claims that the fullness of God is involved in suffering love. Creation involves suffering in God's struggle against the power of the *nihil*. Can this be so in process philosophy? Rooted in relativity physics, can one speak of creation not only as a self-giving act but as an act also involving suffering? In a profound sense, one can. God creates by feeling every element of creation as it has felt itself. In process parlance, this is not an option for God; it is essential to the very nature of God. It is the nature of God to feel every other as it has become and as its future might yet be. Out of these feelings, integrated by God into the depths of the divine nature, God generates new possibilities for the ongoing good of the world. Insofar as the world God experiences contains suffering, then God provides ways beyond that suffering by taking that suffering into the divine self. If we leap from process philosophy to Christian history, is this not the great revelation on the cross? Haven't Christians always said that God takes human sin within God's incarnate self for the sake of redeeming us from sin and evil?

Utilizing trinitarian theology, Meeks speaks of God's perfecting work as the work of the Spirit. This, too, involves the self-giving and the suffering of God. Within a process framework, saving the world is for the sake of perfecting the world within God and in the ongoing history of the world. Eschatologically, the world is perfected as it is taken into God's own self in a work of judgment and transformation that finally draws the world into conformity with God. Yet as Whitehead notes, that which is done in heaven feeds back into the ongoing possibilities for the world. Out of the world's integration within God come transforming possibilities for the ongoing world, reflecting as much as possible under conditions of finitude the very nature of God. God's nature is fundamentally self-giving, empathic, relational. The reflection of God's nature in history is exemplified most fully in communities of inclusive well-being. Process philosophy does not use trinitarian language. Yet the qualities attributed to God in Meeks's thoroughly trinitarian *God the Economist* are philosophically grounded most fully within process philosophy.

For both Meeks and a process analysis of existence, apart from the presence of God there would be no world. Apart from the presence of God there would be no redemption, no moving from destruction to resurrection. Apart from the presence of God there would be no resolution to the world's sorrows beyond the tragedies of history. Apart from the presence of God, there would be no presence at all. With the presence of God there is creation, redemption, perfection. With the presence of God, there is a power for justice in the world.

On the basis of the deep consonance between the theological vision Meeks develops in *God the Economist* and the philosophical vision developed by Alfred North Whitehead, I suggest that we recognize this consonance by giving Meeks a new title. He is indeed a biblical theologian and a trinitarian theologian. He can be called a liberation theologian, and a theologian in the tradition of Moltmann's theology of hope. He is also M. Douglas Meeks: Process Theologian.

7

Christology in the Context of Current Western Systematic Theological Reflection

MICHAEL WELKER

For most of the twentieth century, Christology, seen from the perspective of Western theology, was in a most complicated or even dismal state. In several ways theology was responsible for this development, as it distorted and blocked serious christological thought. There was a broad consensus in the academic community that we have no knowledge of the pre-Easter life of Jesus Christ. The "new quest for the historical Jesus," now known as the "second quest for the historical Jesus," resulted in a total historical skepticism, which claimed that we do not know the historical Jesus but have him only in "legendary portraits." On this basis—that is, without clear perspectives on the historical Jesus—the problem arose that the crucified, resurrected and elevated Christ could not gain contours either.

In addition, the cross of Christ was associated with the suffering God only. Bonhoeffer's powerful statement that "only the suffering God can help" was repeated by leading theologians of different schools. It often seemed to carry this message: "It is only through His suffering that God can help." Yet it was not clear at all how this help was to be conceived. Finally, there was a constant battle concerning the resurrection, which was perceived as resuscitation and reanimation, an understanding affirmed by fundamentalists and ridiculed by skeptics. Behind the heated battle between the two equally misleading positions it remained totally unclear how a merely resuscitated Jesus could become the Lord and Savior of the world. Both sides, existentialists and supernaturalists, became easy targets for a critique of religion in general and of resurrection thought in particular.

The last thirty years, however, have ended this agonizing situation. A "third quest for the historical Jesus" started to change the landscape of Jesus research. The discussion of the theology of the cross in connection with work on the historical Jesus and his time, a period dominated by the global Roman power, opened new perspectives on the revelatory potential of the crucifixion.[1] Moreover, the discourse of systematic theology with biblical scholars on the one hand and with scientists on the other led to freeing insights into the spiritual reality of the resurrection.[2]

In the following, I propose that in the light of these developments we can and should, first, once again focus on the teaching of the *munus triplex Christi*—the threefold office of Christ—in order to renew christological thinking in the West and beyond. The differentiation of the three offices or the threefold office, which can occasionally be found in the church fathers, reached the status of a dogmatic teaching in Calvin's *Institutes*, book two, chapter 15. Here Calvin states, "To know the purpose for which Christ was sent by the Father, and what he conferred upon us, we must look above all at three things in Him, the prophetic office, kingship and priesthood." Calvin develops a biblically based teaching of Christ's threefold saving activity, first the prophetic office, second the kingly office, and finally the priestly office.[3]

Edmund Schlink observed in his *Ecumenical Dogmatics* that the spreading of the doctrine of the threefold office of Christ is a unique ecumenical phenomenon.[4] It reached its dogmatic shape not before but after the separation of the churches, and yet it became common teaching in the different confessional traditions. Through Johann Gerhard's nine-volume work *Loci theologici* (1610–22, IV, 15), this teaching was taken up by Lutheran dogmatics and transported into the nineteenth century by Schleiermacher's *Glaubenslehre*. In the twentieth century, it reached virtually all confessions and churches. Josef Scheeben implemented it in the Catholic traditions.[5] Vatican II made ample use of it, and also in Orthodox dogmat-

1. Welker, *What Happens in Holy Communion?*; Smit, "'. . . Under Pontius Pilate,'" 19–49; and Smit, *Essays in Public Theology*.

2. Polkinghorne and Welker, *The End of the World and the Ends of God*; Peters et al., *Resurrection*; Eckstein and Welker, *Die Wirklichkeit der Auferstehung*.

3. Calvin, *Institutes*, 1:494–503.

4. Schlink, *Ökumenische Dogmatik*, 414f.

5. Scheeben, *Handbuch*, part 5, 2.

ics (cf. Schlink) it gained an important place. In an emergent way it became ecumenical consensus not only in the Reformation churches but also in the broad run from the Orthodox to the Pentecostal churches.[6] The teaching of the threefold office of Christ allows us to focus clearly on the public Christ in different domains of life, and it allows us to differentiate and to relate Christ's presence in ecclesial, political, and moral contexts.[7]

Two additional moves are crucial in order to gain the full impact of this dogmatic orientation. The first of these further moves is already present in Calvin's *Institutes*. With reference to Isa 61:1–2 and Luke 4:18, Calvin states, "We see that he [Christ] was anointed by the Spirit . . . not only for himself that he might carry on the office of teaching, but for the whole body that the power of the Spirit might be present in the continuing preaching of the Gospel."[8] Calvin stressed an insight that had already become most important in early Christianity: Jesus Christ is not only the one on whom the Spirit of God rests; Jesus Christ pours the Spirit to constitute his post-Easterly body. He pours the Spirit in order to live in his witnesses and to allow his witnesses to live in him.[9]

The second additional move is concerned with the different offices of Christ. How do we avoid all sorts of arbitrary constructions of the three offices? How do we avoid the danger that all sorts of religious and moral ideas shape our view of the offices of Christ according to our own possibly contingent desires and needs? In short, how do we avoid the problem that Christ is functionalized or even ideologized? In my view, the most helpful recommendations propose that we orient the three offices of Christ with respect to his pre-Easter life, his cross, and his resurrection.[10]

What can the pre-Easter life of Jesus contribute to the teaching of the three offices? The clear awareness of the multidimensionality of the real life of Jesus Christ opened up totally new potentials in the search for the

6. Schlink, *Ökumenische Dogmatik*, 413f.; or more specifically Macchia, *Justified in the Spirit*, chs. 6 and 9, esp. 169, 174ff., 277. For an Orthodox example, see the analysis of Staniloae by Bartos, *Deification in Eastern Orthodox Theology*, 224f., and Trempelas, *Dogmatik*, 143–203.

7. This has been a key concern of Douglas Meeks in many of his publications from early on. Stackhouse et al., *Christian Social Ethics in a Global Era*; cf. also Schüssler Fiorenza et al., *Politische Theologie*.

8. Calvin, *Institutes*, 1:496.

9. Dunn, "Towards the Spirit of Christ," 3–26.

10. Migliore, *Faith Seeking Understanding*, 186f.; Welker, *Gottes Offenbarung. Christologie (God the Revealed: Christology)*.

historical Jesus and in the orientation derived from it. The search for the historical Jesus and for the radiance of his life, for the constitution of faith and fellowship, has to take into account the likelihood that Jesus had a different impact on the rural population of Galilee than on the urban population of Jerusalem. It must consider the likelihood that all those who resisted the Roman occupation and wished to hold the Mosaic law or the temple cult in high esteem received Jesus differently from those who wanted to embrace the Roman culture. We have to consider the likelihood that those who experienced Jesus' healing and acceptance gave different testimonies than those whose main impression of Jesus was formed in the conflicts with the religious and political forces in Jerusalem. The life of the historical Jesus, which gives rise to and nourishes the multiplicity of memories, expectations, and experiences, leads to different images of Jesus that stand in tension and even in conflict with one another. This refined view of what is historical enables us to see that the desperate reductionist search for the lowest common denominator is a mistaken path. We cannot treat Jesus like a stone in the desert. Historically important and revealing are precisely the differences and tensions among clusters of biblical testimony that nevertheless are in themselves coherent and consistent.

We now see that the real life of Christ radiates into different contexts and thus generates different perspectives on him. One of these perspectives emphasizes the diaconal dimensions. As John Dominic Crossan and others put it, Jesus attended to the basic needs of human beings: nourishment, health, and mutual acceptance.[11] His practice of love and forgiveness, his extension of table fellowship, and an egalitarian ethos characterize his kingly office. This king, who is also a brother and friend, even a poor person and an outcast, shapes the constant movement toward radical democracy characterized by love and care, mutual acceptance, recognition, and respect. In the power of the Spirit, the discipleship of Christ, consciously and unconsciously, gives shape to a reign-of-God movement. This reign has a gigantic impact on the political, social, and cultural life across the earth.[12]

The constant striving for mandatory education and health care in many societies today has to be seen in this light. By the power of the Spirit this office of Christ involves people across the globe and across the centuries. It constitutes one of the three shapes (*drei Gestalten*) of his reign. However, this orientation alone is not sufficient. It can even lead to christological and

11. Crossan, *The Historical Jesus*; Crossan, *Jesus: A Revolutionary Biography*.
12. Meeks, *The Portion of the Poor*.

theological distortions. The prophetic office and the priestly office are of equal importance—indeed, the three offices have to be respected in their perichoretic union.

How do we conceive of the prophetic office and its relation to the cross? The cross of Christ witnesses to a most dramatic situation of the human condition. We, along with other humans and all creation, are bound to finitude, fragility, and the unavoidable brutality of life, all of which lead to the groaning of creation and to the search for God's guidance and God's goals for the world. The deeper and much more dramatic message of the cross is that the good orders and institutions that should support human life, societies, and cultures—including even religion and the church—can be misused, distorted, and transformed into powers of sin, powers of the self-jeopardy of humankind and its disconnection from God.

In his important book *The Crucified God*, Jürgen Moltmann differentiated the message of the cross of Christ by saying that Jesus died in conflict with the Jewish religion as a blasphemer, in conflict with the Roman Empire as an insurgent, and in tension with God in God-forsakenness.[13] I think that this differentiation is most helpful, although it does not cover all the dimensions witnessed to in the biblical message of the cross. Jesus indeed dies in conflict with the Jewish religion, and he dies in conflict with the world power Rome. He also dies in conflict with two types of law—the Jewish and the Roman law—and he dies in conflict with public opinion: "And they cried out again: 'Crucify him' . . . and they shouted all the more: 'Crucify him'" (Mark 15:13ff.; Matt 27:22f.; Luke 23:21f.; John 19:6–15). Jews and Gentiles, friends and foes, indeed the whole world conspires in its resistance against the saving presence of God.

Despite this dramatic message, however, the cross of Christ is a revelatory and salvific event in more ways than one. In light of the resurrection and the work of the pre-Easter Jesus, it is an event that marks a turning point in the world and in the salvation of humanity and all creation. It is not without reason that the cross of Christ stands at the center of the church and stands for the center of Christian faith. Christian piety loses its gravity, its weight, and its orientation when faith no longer comes from the cross and from the crucified Christ.

The cross of Christ reveals the situation of global hopelessness from which there is no escape. It is a situation in which the so-called enemies, the global public, and even the resistance fighters—the disciples—conspire

13. Moltmann, *Crucified God*, ch. 4.

and are implicated.[14] The situation of God-forsakenness here is not only one of individual and collective disorientation. Rather, this situation of God-forsakenness displays itself in global public anomie, in global public chaos, and in a triumph of sin, all of which pervert the good forces of life. Religion, law, politics, and public opinion work together and bring about this situation. The cross reveals the abysmal situation that in the name of justice and the good, in the name of truth and salvation, innocent people can be ostracized, tortured, and killed. The cross reveals the law in all its dimensions under the power of sin. It thus reveals the radical difference between God and humanity. The cross does not reveal the absolute "death of God," but indeed the serious possibility that from this point on God is dead to human beings.

In the light and darkness of the cross of Christ, the prophetic office gains its shape and its depth. A constant critical and self-critical search for truth and justice is generated, and a public proclamation and education is connected with it. This prophetic office is not limited to the realms of the church. In partly or fully secularized forms, it captures truth- and justice-seeking communities in the academy, in the legal system, in education, and in civil societies.[15] The prophetic office can even turn against religious communities and churches. It can be executed in most dramatic forms up to the level of nonviolent resistance and suffering. The unfolding of the message given by these two offices of Christ, the kingly and the prophetic, opens new perspectives for a biblically oriented and realistic Christology and ecclesiology. It also offers a great challenge and task for a global public theology—a theology that many of our colleagues are in search of today.

Finally, we have to focus on the priestly office of Christ, the priestly shape of the reign of God. This office has all too often been limited to the topics of sacrifice and atonement. I propose to seek to unfold its orienting power in the light of the resurrection witnesses. The fragmentary and almost modest character of the witnesses to the resurrection is striking. That may be the reason why the arts have had such difficulty in depicting the event of the resurrection. The biblical witnesses contradict the few attempts in the fine arts, such as the Isenheim Altarpiece, to represent Jesus the victor as an icon of the resurrection. Rather, the biblical texts speak of testimonies that are characterized on the one hand by personal authenticity

14. Welker, *What Happens in Holy Communion?*; Smit, "'. . . Under Pontius Pilate,'" 19–49; and Smit, *Essays in Public Theology*.

15. Welker and Polkinghorne, *Faith in the Living God*.

and certainty of the experience and on the other hand by its fragmentary, fleeting, and perspectival character, which easily invites doubts and necessitates the search for truth.

Francis Fiorenza has emphasized that this character of testimony, fragmented and perspectival, is indispensable to the resurrection witnesses. He assumes that these necessarily multiple testimonies push toward metaphorical speech when they refer to each other and seek to thematize the complex reality, which they present perspectivally. Above all he has called attention to the fact that these testimonies seek to be anchored in actual and symbolic actions that become basic ritual forms of the early church.[16]

The testimonies to the resurrection are expressed in address, in the breaking of the bread, in the greeting of peace, in the opening of the scriptures, and in other ritual actions and signs. These expressions form the basic life of the early church. This somewhat fragile theophany, mediated through proclamation, the opening of the messiah-secret in the scriptures, the celebration of Holy Communion, the sending of the disciples, and the command to baptize—this is what is witnessed to by the resurrection accounts of the biblical traditions. This view paves the way toward an understanding of the reign of God and of the reign of the resurrected Christ as an emergent reality. Out of a structured and definite multiplicity of witnesses the resurrected Lord edifies and shapes his church. Powerful monohierarchical forms in the history of the church, with its splendid feasts and great cathedrals, should not tempt us to overlook the fact that the power of Christ's Spirit is operative in a different way. Emergent processes with a polyphony of witnesses to the triune God's creative presence constitute the reign of Christ in his evolving church.

With the breaking of the bread and the disclosure of the messiah-secret, the resurrection witnesses clearly relate to the second dimension, the cross of Christ and its deep conflict with what scripture often calls "the world." In each celebration of Holy Communion a deeply distressing memory of this dimension of Christ's life and suffering is re-enacted. Jesus celebrates communion with Peter, who repeatedly denies him, and with the disciples, who fall asleep although he has asked them to stay awake with him and who finally forsake him and flee. He even celebrates communion with Judas, although he speaks the words of woe against him. The breaking of the bread indicates Jesus' and God's deepest merciful care for those who

16. Schüssler Fiorenza, "Resurrection of Jesus," 213ff.

disconnect themselves from the presence of God. It shows the depth of the divine forgiveness of sins.[17]

Here we encounter the sacrificial love of God, who continues to forgive us and save us despite the victimization of Jesus Christ by humans.[18] The priestly office clearly relates to the kingly office. It witnesses to God's will that humans constitute not only symbolic table fellowship but also a community of mutual acceptance and mutual care, of justice and peace. Yet the priestly office reveals and conveys even more than that. It reveals a God who shows his mercy not only by healing and restituting human life but also by elevating and ennobling it. In this way the priestly office serves the cognition, adoration, and glorification of the true and living God, who shows his mercy by elevating creation to divine glory. With the priestly office the definitely ecclesial responsibilities and loyalties of a christologically oriented theology come into view. In this dimension we stand in continuity with the Augsburg Confession VII and the Reformation catechisms.

This stance does not mean that the main task of a theology that focuses on the priestly office would be to strengthen a specific institutionalized form of the church for its own sake. The main task of the priestly office and the priestly shape of the reign is to witness in proclamation, liturgy, teaching, and mission to the sustaining, saving, and ennobling God. This God is also present in the loving kingly office and in the truth- and justice-seeking prophetic office and shape of the divine reign. With respect to the threefold shape of the reign of Christ we can affirm Christ's divinity without mere metaphysical speculations. The resurrected and elevated Christ reveals that God seeks nothing less than to win his creatures for a share in his own life and glory. The priestly office conveys this salvific message and revelation. We have to notice at this point that theology has to rise to the challenge to understand itself not only as a contextual theology, not only as a public theology, and not only as a theology concerned with contemporary world Christianity. In the light of the priestly office of Christ, theology should try to become a truly ecumenical and eschatological theology—without losing its concrete moral, political, and global responsibilities and virtues.[19]

17. Welker, *What Happens in Holy Communion?*, chs. 2 and 10.

18. Brandt, *Opfer als Gedächtnis.*

19. A book edited by Meeks, *Trinity, Community, and Power*, seeks a similar approach in a Trinitarian orientation.

Bibliography

Bartos, Emil. *Deification in Eastern Orthodox Theology: An Evaluation and Critique of the Theology of Dumitru Staniloae.* Milton Keynes: Paternoster, 2002.

Brandt, Sigrid. *Opfer als Gedächtnis. Auf dem Weg zu einer befreienden theologischen Rede von Opfer.* Münster: LIT, 2001.

Calvin, John. *Institutes of the Christian Religion.* Edited by John T. McNeill. Translated by Ford Lewis Battles. 2 vols. Library of Christian Classics 20–21. Philadelphia: Westminster, 1960.

Crossan, John Dominic. *The Historical Jesus: The Life of a Mediterranean Jewish Peasant.* Edinburgh: T. & T. Clark, 1991.

———. *Jesus: A Revolutionary Biography.* New York: HarperCollins, 1995.

Dunn, James. "Towards the Spirit of Christ: The Emergence of the Distinctive Features of Christian Pneumatology." In *The Work of the Spirit: Pneumatology and Pentecostalism,* edited by Michael Welker, 3–26. Grand Rapids: Eerdmans, 2006.

Eckstein, Hans-Joachim, and Michael Welker. *Die Wirklichkeit der Auferstehung.* Neukirchen-Vluyn: Neukirchener, 2002.

Macchia, Frank D. *Justified in the Spirit: Creation, Redemption, and the Triune God.* Grand Rapids: Eerdmans, 2010.

Meeks, M. Douglas, ed. *The Portion of the Poor: Good News to the Poor in the Wesleyan Tradition.* Nashville: Kingswood, 1995.

———, ed. *Trinity, Community, and Power: Mapping Trajectories in Wesleyan Theology.* Nashville: Kingswood, 2000.

Migliore, Daniel. *Faith Seeking Understanding: An Introduction to Christian Theology.* Grand Rapids: Eerdmans, 2004.

Moltmann, Jürgen. *The Crucified God.* Translated by R. A. Wilson and John Bowden. Minneapolis: Fortress, 1993.

Peters, Ted, et al., eds. *Resurrection. Theological and Scientific Assessments.* Grand Rapids: Eerdmans, 2002.

Polkinghorne, John, and Michael Welker, eds. *The End of the World and the Ends of God: Science and Theology on Eschatology.* Harrisburg, PA: Trinity, 2000.

Scheeben, Matthias. *Handbuch katholischer Dogmatik.* 2nd ed. Freiburg: Herder, 1954.

Schlink, Edmund. *Ökumenische Dogmatik: Grundzüge.* Göttingen: Vandenhoeck & Ruprecht, 1985.

Schüssler Fiorenza, Francis. "The Resurrection of Jesus in Roman Catholic Fundamental Theology." In *The Resurrection: An Interdisciplinary Symposium on the Resurrection of Jesus,* edited by Stephen T. Davis et al., 213–48. Oxford: Oxford University Press, 1997.

Schüssler Fiorenza, Francis, et al. *Politische Theologie. Neuere Geschichte und Potenziale.* Neukirchen-Vluyn: Neukirchener, 2011. In English, *Political Theology: Contemporary Challenges and Future Directions.* Louisville: Westminster John Knox, 2013.

Smit, Dirk. *Essays in Public Theology: Collected Essays 1.* Stellenbosch, South Africa: Sun, 2007.

———. "'. . . Under Pontius Pilate': On Living Cultural Memory and Christian Confession." In *Who is Jesus Christ for Us Today? Pathways to Contemporary Christology,* edited by Andreas Schuele and Günter Thomas, 19–49. Louisville: Westminster John Knox, 2009.

Stackhouse, Max L., et al. *Christian Social Ethics in a Global Era.* Nashville: Abingdon, 1995.

Trempelas, Panagiōtēs. *Dogmatikē: tēs Orthodoxou Katholikēs Ekklēsias.* 3 vols. Athens: Zōē, 1959–61.

Welker, Michael. *Gottes Offenbarung. Christologie.* Neukirchen-Vluyn: Neukirchener, 2012. In English, *God the Revealed: Christology.* Grand Rapids: Eerdmans, 2013.

———. *What Happens in Holy Communion?* Grand Rapids: Eerdmans, 2000.

Welker, Michael, and John Polkinghorne. *Faith in the Living God. A Dialogue.* Philadelphia: Fortress, 2001.

8

Interpreting the Text, Interpreting the World: A Wesleyan Hermeneutics of Economic Life

SONDRA WHEELER

Introduction

The self-consciousness of a postmodern age has taught us to see ourselves as agents in our own readings of texts and to recognize that we read inescapably as twenty-first-century Africans or North Americans or what have you, caught up in our own questions and shaped by our own societies. Yet it is something of a jolt to see our theological ancestors, even the primary sources of our common tradition, every bit as constructively engaged in making meaning out of the biblical text. Particularly for those of us who are Methodists, it may be illuminating as well as unsettling to see John Wesley for the supremely active reader and expositor he was.

Wesley read the Bible as an Englishman in the eighteenth century, at the cusp of political and economic transformations whose future consequences were still below the horizon and unimaginable. He read the canonical texts with, to, and for other Englishmen and women—and their half-alienated offspring in the New World—his interpretation and application moving with the ease of unselfconsciousness between first-century Palestine and eighteenth-century London. He read preeminently as a pastor engaged in forming and sustaining a community, with an eye always to the needs and circumstances and sins of his own people. None of this is to fault him as a reader; it is merely to note that his reading was shaped by his situation and driven (as all readings are) by his purposes, which are always more than exegetical.

This observation would not have troubled Wesley in the least. It was for him a fundamental and orienting point of doctrine that scripture was the most purposive of books, written to awaken in humanity a fear of God's judgment and a hope of God's mercy. The preacher's task is to bring the two-edged sword of God's word to bear upon a particular community for the sake of their salvation. It is hard to know what Wesley would have made of our notion of exegesis as a neutral, scientific, and historical unpacking of an ancient text that seeks neither to edify one's soul nor to guide and instruct the souls of one's fellows. It seems likely he would have thought such "interpretation" no business of a minister of the gospel.

My aim in what follows is to review and reconsider the body of Wesley's material concerning the use of possessions and the terms on which Christians participate in the world of labor, production, and exchange. I am looking in particular for the strategies by which, and the ends to which, he turns to biblical texts to address his people and the structures that ordered their material lives. This task seems like a fitting way to honor the long labor of Doug Meeks, who has done so much to open our eyes to the way in which the logic of modern economics has rendered the Bible's assumptions about the sustenance of human lives and communities not only inoperative but nearly invisible, even for those of us whose work is centered in the critical interpretation of this canon. Perhaps we can find guidance and inspiration in the model offered by Wesley, an interpreter whose gaze is penetrating and whose proclamation is unflinching.

In the space available, it will not be possible to deal exhaustively with Wesley's writing on these topics. Nevertheless, this is not an area in which we see a great deal of shift and development in the substance of Wesley's thought but only a gradual darkening of his expectation that the preached word will fall on hearing ears. The portion dealt with here should be able fairly to reflect the whole.

Primary Sources

As is well known, Wesley devotes a substantial amount of ink to the subject of money, returning to it several times, using a variety of biblical passages as his launching points. At the same time, it is important not to distort the place of this subject in the whole sweep of Wesley's preaching and writing.

However striking and memorable this strand of his work may be and how-ever important it may be for us to attend to, it represents the central focus of only a small percentage of texts. Notably, though, the chronology of those texts suggests an increasing focus on possessions as a moral and spiritual danger, and an increasing urgency to his concerns, as Wesley observed the course of his Societies' development. Near the end of his life, these issues seemed to haunt him, causing him to call into question the fruitfulness of his whole ministry.

The standard list of pertinent works will be familiar even to casual students of Wesley's thought. Listed in chronological order, the most widely known (and equally widely misrepresented) sermon is "The Use of Money" (1744), followed by "The Good Steward" (1758), "The Danger of Riches" (1780), and one called simply "On Riches" (1788). In addition, there is the deeply disappointed sermon "On the Causes of the Inefficacy of Christian-ity" (1789) as well as the final, almost desperate "On the Danger of Increas-ing Riches" (1790). Also relevant is the pamphlet "Thoughts on the Present Scarcity of Provisions" (1773), notable for its generality of address and its attention to the systematic effects of individual decisions and practices. Brief remarks about the potency, usefulness, and peril of wealth are laced through dozens of other sermons as occasion arises—for example, in his multiple treatments of the Sermon on the Mount. However, none of these develops points not already represented in the works cited above. Thus it seems safe, at least as an initial appraisal, to focus on what exactly Wesley is busy interpreting in each of the standard sources and what central interpre-tive strategies govern his readings.

The Use of Money:
Competition, Consumption, and Accumulation

Wesley's sermon "The Use of Money" has been a victim of its popularity, or more precisely of its homiletical effectiveness. It takes up a text that has confused and embarrassed the church for centuries, the Parable of the Un-just Steward (Luke 16:1–13), and handily transforms it into three easily remembered maxims. Moreover, on first glance these do not seem all that challenging. The first of his "three plain rules" is that we should "gain all we can." Embedded as we are in our own happily acquisitive society, this seems to us a little like admonishing fire to burn or water to be wet; but of course, Wesley has just begun. By the time he has finished his exposition of all the means and terms of gain that are ruled out for Christians, the force of this injunction appears quite different. He has excluded anything that harms the believer in body, mind, or spirit, anything that saps health or perverts character or weakens faith and joy in God. He also excludes anything that harms the neighbor in any aspect, by damaging her body, by failing to exercise due diligence in her protection, or by exploiting her weaknesses of mind or failings of character: anything that involves or even conduces to one's own or another's sin is out of bounds. This is already a stunning check to business as usual in Wesley's day, as it would be in our own.

Yet these strictures, which according to Wesley are entailed by our duty to love our neighbors as ourselves, are not the most surprising or the most provocative of his instructions. Included in Wesley's explication of what duty forbids are several things we would take for granted as part of healthy competition or the efficient operation of the market and regard as inseparable from capitalism. Wesley says we may not harm our neighbor's substance. Under this heading he rules out not only predatory lending practices, price gouging, and profiting from another's hardship, as well as routine competitive practices. He expressly forbids the sale of goods below market value for the purpose of driving others out of business and lays it down as a general principle that we may not "study to ruin our neighbor's trade in order to advance our own" (I-3). He also argues that Christians cannot compete with others for the capacity to do business: they cannot solicit their neighbor's workers or even agree to hire them if in need of them. (He does not appear to have considered competition for labor a potentially positive force in securing livable wages for laborers.) To the extent that competition in trade is constructed as a zero-sum game in which my benefit depends upon your loss, Wesley regards it as contrary to Christian duty.

What is evident here is Wesley's resistance to social and economic changes that were part of the transition from a fundamentally rural and agrarian society toward an urban and manufacturing economy, the prototype of early industrial capitalism. The subject of his interpretation is less the biblical text than his own society: its emerging patterns of commerce and the ethos they were fostering. Wesley regarded the kind of direct competition for a limited market that we take for granted as the basic mechanism of capitalism as a violation of human solidarity, a transgression of our basic duty not to harm. As such, he called into question the whole mechanism for profit-seeking itself.

It is important to note the biblical text that governs Wesley's ethic of commerce is not his ostensible sermon text, the parable of the dishonest steward. This passage receives only scant attention, and that confined to the introductory paragraphs. As the foregoing has already suggested, the true governing text is the oft-repeated and much more central commandment to "love your neighbor as yourself." Christians are to prosper in business by sheer diligence, by ingenuity and excellence in the use of their various skills, and by the superior quality of their work. Anything else violates the commandment "on which hang all the law and the prophets." This Wesley equates with "gaining the world at the cost of your soul." This hermeneutical judgment does the real moral work in this part of the sermon.

Wesley's second rule about saving all one can is not just a plea for modesty or prudence in expenditures. It is an attack upon all the elective consumption that fuels a capitalist society. Licit expenses include those needed to provide basic sustenance for oneself and one's dependents, but Wesley's exposition makes clear that the accent here falls upon "basic." One may in conscience spend enough to support health and strength but not to provide such ancillary benefits as mere variety or pleasure or beauty in one's food, clothing, or surroundings. All these in common are accounted luxuries. Not only do such unnecessary expenditures detract from what may be given away, but they are in themselves condemned as a species of worldliness. Resources devoted to such things are not merely wasted; they are devoted to "the lust of the flesh and the lust of the eyes and the pride of life" (1 John 2:16). This Johannine phrase is used by Wesley repeatedly, in this sermon and elsewhere, to sweep up the motives that drive consumption of whatever is desired without being strictly needed for life. The result is a standard for what may be innocently spent not much beyond bare necessity, with whatever is left over being owed to the poor.

The weight of Wesley's biblical interpretation falls on this identification of unnecessary purchases with "loving the world and the things that are in the world," which Wesley sees as inherently at odds with loving God. The creation of new conveniences and the turning of a newly emerging productive capacity to consumer goods that marked the latter half of the eighteenth century (and which continues as the central economic engine of our own prosperity) becomes on this view one vast temptation. Two-thirds of the way through this first sermon, already the basic premises of consumer capitalism, unfettered market competition, and continuously rising consumption are identified from Wesley's standpoint as manifestations of sin. It is a form of sin that Wesley identifies as mortal, while rejecting the Scholastic category.

Only from this position is it possible to understand what Wesley meant by his third rule, when he told his people to "give all you can." After diligent and disciplined labor, after the most careful management of time and resources, after the studied repudiation of any form of consumption not needed for health and basic self-sustenance, every penny not required for the maintenance of the household was to be devoted to the needs of the poor. This was not charity but simple duty. God, to whom all things belong, had graciously enabled his people to provide for their needs, and now the needs of all beyond the household were waiting to be supplied. Despite its reputation as the most accommodating of Wesley's treatments of wealth, "The Use of Money" takes as its subject not the biblical text but the economics of the emerging Industrial Revolution, which does not fare well.

The Good Steward: Ownership

The sermon called "The Good Steward" uses for its underlying text a single phrase (Luke 16:2b) from the same parable, that of the unjust steward. Now, however, Wesley's interest was turned in a new direction, one that gives this the broadest scope of all his sermons dealing with money. In this address he aims to sum up by one phrase the whole situation of the human being, the whole tenor and shape of Christian duty, and with it the nature of human infidelity. Moreover, he says as much in his introduction, going on to occupy the first third of the sermon with his exposition of the breadth of application of this central metaphor. We are stewards of our souls, bodies, minds, affections, lives, strength, powers, talents, and goods (I:2–8). Certainly the topic of money and possessions is embraced in this list and given attention here, but here as well we find Wesley's most comprehensive account of the dimensions and demands of stewardship.

From this basic theological anthropology comes a picture of moral life both compelling and daunting: everything is owed, no act is morally indifferent, and there can be no works of supererogation, since we can never do more than is our duty. Wesley's concluding gloss on the mild-seeming verse "every man shall receive his own reward according to his own labor" is as follows: "We cannot be wise stewards unless we labor to the uttermost of our power, not leaving anything undone which we can possibly do" (IV, 3). This is nothing less than an interpretation of moral existence.

In this overarching context, the treatment of possessions is wholly consistent but also utterly radical in its implications. Wesley takes the term "steward" in its fullest and most literal sense: a steward is a servant, most often a slave, charged with the administration of another's property. The steward has no stake and no right in what is dispensed and when all has been administered according to the owner's and master's will, then only basic justice has been done.

At the root of Wesley's treatment of ownership is a theological counterpoint to John Locke's labor theory of property, which was highly influential at the time. Locke famously held that a person naturally owns himself and his labor, so that the labor expended to obtain, modify, or make use of a natural resource, including land, gave one a natural right of property in it. Wesley, however, begins with the premise that raw nature, including the human being in his natural state, is not, as Locke assumed, unowned. Rather, God as Creator and Sustainer of all that exists maintains an essential and inalienable claim upon everything.

Thus, neither our bodies nor our labor may be thought of as our own, since we ourselves are God's. Our every capacity comes to us as a trust, an endowment for whose use we are directly accountable to our Maker. We may have used our strength and skills and energy to acquire property and make it beneficial; yet the property, along with the capacities that secured it and the profit that comes of it, together with ourselves, all belong in their entirety to God. God mercifully gives us the privilege of being the first to be served by the goods we hold in trust and the blessing of being givers rather than merely recipients of the fruit of our labor. Still, nothing on earth belongs to us, and for the use of every resource of nature, time, and talent we are wholly accountable before God.

This conviction is in part entailed by the doctrine of creation. Yet Wesley's insistence that the goods of earth are neither gifts nor loans but merely temporary entrustments takes its force from a passage later in Luke, one to which he repeatedly alludes but which he never quotes directly: "If you have not been faithful in the unrighteous mammon, who will entrust you with true riches? And if you have not been faithful in that which is another's, who will give you that which is your own?" (Luke 16:11–12). On Wesley's reading, those things we are used to calling our possessions are by definition "what belongs to another," while those that genuinely belong to us are so only proleptically; they are the spiritual goods waiting in the eternal country for which this present "land of our sojourning" is only test and preparation (I:1).

Thus Wesley's understanding of possessions and their use is grounded at least as much in eschatology as in creation. The rigor and consistency of his standards for legitimate expenses arise partly from the notion of entrustment and the here-and-now practicalities of human needs that our material resources might meet. Yet to an even greater extent, they are determined by the eschatological horizon against which he interprets the most routine transactions. With every expenditure, we are declaring which home we are looking toward and staking a claim to the country of our final dwelling place.

The Danger of Riches: Wealth and Its Seductions

The sermon "The Danger of Riches" is notable in this company for the degree to which it actually focuses on the exposition of the sermon text, 1 Tim 6:9: "They that will be rich fall into a temptation and a snare, and into many foolish and hurtful desires which drown men in destruction and perdition." Wesley allows this text to structure his whole sermon; he proceeds by identifying those who fall under the warning, then details the nature and operation of the threat, and ends with a plea that his hearers turn from destruction.

From the preceding verse, "having food and raiment, with these let us be content" (1 Tim 6:8), Wesley moves summarily to the judgment that all who desire more than this, all who seek it, and even all those who simply retain it when it comes to them without being sought, belong under the rubric of "those who would be rich." This is true whether the wealth is stored as possessions, as land, or as money laid by against adversity. All those who make such provisions, along with all who love money in itself, fall into the temptations and disasters here ascribed to those who desire wealth. On this contention hang the force and persuasiveness of Wesley's whole interpretation and the cogency of the conclusions he draws from it.

Along with what he calls the "gross and unnatural sin of love of money" itself (I, 6), Wesley speaks of the more refined sin of "desiring more" (I, 7). He observes that this desire kept within proper bounds can be innocent, yet notes "how difficult it is not to exceed them!" The danger of riches, plainly put, is sin. Wesley identifies the heart of that peril bluntly: at its root, the sin consists in the desiring of happiness in something other than God

(I, 12). Here Wesley gives his most extensive explication of the Johannine triad comprising love of the world that wars with the love of God.

In fact, much of the sermon explores what a modern commentator might call the psychology of desire. It details the effect of gratifying desires, which is not to quiet but rather to increase them (I, 16). Wesley expounds the experience of ensnarement and the slide into spiritual paralysis and blindness that attends it. He does not merely parse the movements of the passage; he provides a kind of phenomenology of the captivity of affluence. Those who have the means and use them to gratify their desires risk becoming unable to forego them. They are enchained to novelty and ease and convenience; and the blows to patience, humility, zeal, and ultimately to faith and charity that come of that attachment are deadly. This is Wesley as pathologist, describing the natural history of a fatal disease. Indeed, he ends the sermon with a long list of diagnostic questions, inviting his hearers to determine whether they are not infected with this toxic desire that distorts hope, dilutes faith, and destroys zeal for the active work of charity. His concluding word is the warning of Matt 19:24 about how difficult it is for the rich to enter the kingdom.

Here Wesley picks up in the 1788 sermon "On Riches," exploring another dimension of the perilous quality of wealth: the number of temptations to and occasions for sin that lie in the path of the rich. Beginning with the temptation to place one's confidence in riches rather than God, Wesley goes on to describe the particular moral deformities he observes in English social life that reinforce and exacerbate that tendency. He notes how the adjective "good" is applied to any man who is rich, and that a wealthy man is for that reason alone held in honor. He declares it impossible that such a one should escape pride to come to God as the merest sinner, trusting only in faith for salvation, unless by the powerful grace of God. Lacking that realization of a divine welcome altogether unmerited, the rich are hindered in their love for God itself. Should that obstacle be overcome, another waits; for Wesley wonders, "how is it possible for a man not to love the world who is surrounded by all its allurements?" (I-2). Like the rich man of the passage (Matt 19:24), he says, his great possessions will expel the love of God from his soul. Thus faith and love toward God are both wounded.

The acquisition of moral virtues is likewise made more difficult for the rich, for they are "cut off from that freedom of conversation whereby they might be made sensible of their defects, and come to a true knowledge of themselves" (I-4). Surrounded by dependents and sycophants, by those who from fear or greed will offer only flattery, "his situation necessarily occasions praise to flow in upon him from every quarter" (II-5). Wealth ensures that whims are gratified on every side, Wesley observes, as all strive to oblige the wealthy, increasing his self-will and thwarting the development of patience, till he be "ill able to submit to the will of either God or men" (II-6). The rich are thus deprived of opportunities to learn meekness and gentleness, to learn to yield to other persons, and to love with disinterested benevolence those who do not flatter and pamper their vanity. Not only the love of God but the love of neighbor will find little occasion to grow up in such a setting. More than an interpretation of the passage, this is an interpretation and critique of British society, of the moral distortions Wesley saw embedded in its class-conscious social order.

Speaking at last not to the rich in general but to the wealthy now among his own congregations, Wesley applies to them the words of Jas 5:1: "Woe to you rich, weep and howl for the miseries which are coming upon you." Here Wesley is no longer principally interpreting scripture, whether in particular or in whole. He is no longer expounding the divine purpose of money or the deep theological aptness of the metaphor of stewardship or the wide parameters and insidious power of the lusts of the flesh. Now he begins to deal with the failure of his decades of preaching and teaching to counter the effects of the changing social location of Methodists on their lives, their conduct, and their souls. With their growth in property, status, respectability, and wealth, he sees them falling prey to all that his analysis of desire and the temptations of riches could predict but has not been able to prevent.

Inefficacy and Increasing Wealth:
The Captive State of the Church

In the sermon "On the Causes of the Inefficacy of Christianity," Wesley undertakes to interpret just that fact. In a long and awkward prelude, he declares the inhabitants of the greater part of the world, including most of Christendom, to be ignorant heathens. Yet they are not Wesley's chief concern or the source of his grief, and he does not linger long on their situation. Instead, he grapples with the lack of evidence of spiritual progress he sees among those who have the benefit of both sound Christian doctrine and clear Christian discipline: those of his own congregations. He sets out to interpret the internal dynamics of decay and corruption within the Methodist movement and attributes it to the failure of the practices of self-denial among them. The Methodists' behavior in the use of money is in a sense merely an example of that larger pattern. However, corruption related to wealth receives his most sustained attention, both beginning and ending the analysis of the disease and decay he finds within his churches.

Wesley reports that many in his charge observe the first rule of gaining all they can, fewer observe that of saving all they can, but hardly any observe the rule of giving all they can, while it is for the sake of this that the other two are promulgated. This truncated financial prudence, he declares, leaves them "twofold more the children of hell than they were before" (8). With a candor that is painful to confront, Wesley admits his own perplexity and his regrets: "I am distressed. I know not what to do. . . . With regard to dress, I might have been as firm (and I now see it would have been far better) as the people called Quakers, or the Moravian Brethren. . . . But alas! The time is now past; and what I can do now I cannot tell" (12).

Wesley traces the terrible irony that makes even the gifts of divine grace (sobriety, diligence, self-restraint, and discipline) agents of self-destruction; for this is what they become when they are severed from the goal of holiness they are given to serve and turned merely to the service of prosperity. The only remedy, Wesley insists, is the rigorous restraint that rules out all unnecessary expense: "I can see only one way . . . if you have any desire to escape the damnation of hell, then give all you can" (18).

That brings us to the last of these central texts, Wesley's final cry against what he has come to see as the bitter end of the revival he has worked for throughout his lifetime. All the themes of "The Danger of Increasing Riches" are familiar. Indeed, much of its wording paraphrases portions of earlier sermons. What is different here is the tone. The rhetoric is sharper, the intensity greater than ever before. If not quite despairing, the sermon may fairly be called desperate in its plea that those who have increased in wealth not use that as the occasion for richer living or idleness or any other form of self-indulgence, lest they abandon the faith and imperil their own souls.

Clear and explicit here is Wesley's conviction that salvation itself rests upon faithfulness in the use of money. If there is anything new to note, it is the weight of eschatological expectation (both in hope and in fear) conveyed in this sermon. This is not inconsistent with Wesley's earliest writing, but long observation has darkened his expectations of a positive response at the same time as it has increased the urgency of his preaching. One has here the sense that the near approach of his own death moves him to fear, not for himself, but for the spiritual health and indeed the survival of his movement. Like Moses' final discourse at the edge of the Jordan in Deuteronomy, this is a last cry to those whom he fears will perish, ensnared by the very bounty God has provided: "Turn and live!"

Thoughts on the Present Scarcity of Provisions: Toward Interpreting the World

For all his intense focus upon preaching and pastoral leadership, Wesley did not restrict his hermeneutical work to the interpretation of texts or to the moral and spiritual state of his religious societies. In his pamphlet on the roots of scarcity, he confronted the desperate and widespread poverty affecting England in his day and searched for causes. He was groping for the means of systematic economic analysis, a science then in its infancy. Without either the mathematical tools or the data that would enable later thinkers to trace large-scale trends and delineate complex relationships, still Wesley looked for patterns that explained why problems existed and how they might most effectively be attacked. In this brief tract, he offered the fruit of his analysis.

Historical context is helpful in this instance. Beginning late in the seventeenth century and continuing throughout Wesley's lifetime, an increasing proportion of arable and grazing land once held in common had been fenced off and given by title to individual owners under the Enclosure Acts. Those who had been subsistence farmers were displaced, and as land values increased many of the smallest landholders were priced out of the market. This left former farm families in need of livelihood at the same time that it drove down the price of labor by concentrating unskilled workers in the cities, to which they flocked in search of jobs.

Years of experience among the poor made Wesley an extraordinarily well-informed observer of those effects, as a whole segment of the population was deprived of access to the most basic subsistence. Changing land use patterns, as well as the cost of transporting, storing, and distributing food commodities, made the price of foodstuffs higher in cities. On top of everything else, he insists, the widespread production of distilled alcohol and the keeping of numerous horses by the wealthy deflected much of the harvest of grain, driving up the price of that portion left for food, leaving the poor unable to buy bread. Even for the moderately well-off, high food

prices constricted resources for other purchases, resulting in business con-
tractions and failures that contributed to even higher levels of unemployment. In this pamphlet, Wesley testified to the brutal want and outright
starvation that came of it.

Wesley also decried the high tax burdens of his time as a weight on
commerce, blaming that burden partly on smuggling and tax evasion and
partly on wasteful government expenses that served the interests of the
few at the expense of the many. Unemployment is the proximate cause of
destitution, Wesley argued, and he found the roots of unemployment in
luxury and the misuse of goods, in high taxes resulting from tax evasion
and abuse, and in self-serving policies pursued by the powerful.

Thus, Wesley denounced as "wickedly and devilishly false" the com-
monplace claim that the poor were poor only because they were lazy or
profligate. Instead, he argued, they suffered from the effects of large-scale
changes over which they had no control and from the greed, self-indulgence, and hard-heartedness of the upper classes. Wesley made quite clear
the moral and spiritual implications of this analysis in sermons and instruction for the members of his Societies as well as for the wider public
toward whom this tract was directed. Luxury and the hoarding of resources
were denounced as crimes against God and neighbor. Even the temperance
movement, embraced by the Methodists because of the spread of alcohol-
ism and related social pathologies, had for Wesley this significant economic
aspect: that it attacked an industry he saw as taking bread from the mouths
of the hungry.

Learning from Our Forebears

We see here how John Wesley was engaged in interpreting his texts vigor-
ously and powerfully in light of the circumstances and failings of his own
churches and of the society in which they were embedded. We cannot leave
this topic without asking, What would an analogous hermeneutic look like
in our own world? What are the tasks that face us as expositors of scripture
who are also teachers of the church, observers of the world, and participants in a global conversation about economics and the human good?

Below are several suggestions, each of them of sufficient scale to occupy any number of researchers for multiple years. I offer them merely as
a stimulus to our thinking about what it might involve for us to continue

John Wesley's tradition of broad and unflinching economic, social, and spiritual critique.

- Prevailing in the developed world and rapidly being transferred to the developing world is a system of capitalization, production, and distribution driven by short- and medium-term profit for those with resources to invest. So powerful is this driver that even the long-term stability of publicly held corporations is often sacrificed to it and with that the welfare of employees and eventual users alike. A vigorous analysis of the perverse incentives that undercut effective production and distribution of goods in favor of immediate benefits for the few is a place that theologians and business analysts might find a common starting point.

- Ready transportation and instant communication draw corporations into competition for global markets at the same time they make it possible to move resource acquisition and production anywhere on the planet. The flexibility and power of multinational corporations has outreached control by the political structures of nation-states. The results are vast, including a decline in wages and benefits, the effective evasion of regulations regarding fair labor practices and workplace safety, and the neutralization of environmental protection legislation. Wesley's vigorous critique might bring us to ask fundamental critical questions, such as the following: What are the aims of economic life? What are the measures of a good economic system? What political structures might order a global economy toward the flourishing of the earth and its peoples?

- It is estimated that the average American is exposed to three thousand commercial messages per day. We might devote serious research to the moral and theological analysis of the psychology of desire in a society saturated by a mass media advertising culture. Our whole system lives on the insatiability of desire, indeed on the deliberate and calculated creation of desire for products heretofore nonexistent. This is at once the engine of our affluence and the force hastening the degradation of our environment. What resources does the thought and practice of our faith bring to the runaway train of rising consumption in the West?

- At a deeper level, we might examine the effect upon faith, indeed upon human existence, of a world of continuous distraction. Our modes of stimulation now follow us via earphone and podcast into every mo-ment and every space of our frantic lives. We are constantly enter-tained, via music and images, video and electronic games, so that we need never have an idle moment—or a reflective thought. Do we even recognize an inner life? Or have we rendered ourselves effectively deaf to what Wesley would have called the inward promptings of the Holy Spirit and drowned out the voice of God?

- Finally, Wesley traced the failure of Christian faith to transform lives to his people's unwillingness to practice self-denial. We, meanwhile, have all but lost the language. Can we achieve even the flickers of self-forgetfulness that make it possible to attend to the needs of others? Ours is a culture that has rejected suffering, regarding it not so much as a mystery as an offense, an infringement upon our entitlement to happiness and ease. Are we prepared to read the Bible to and for our own society, prepared to reclaim its insistence that the one who loses his life will save it? Moreover, do we have the imagination to proclaim as good news the message that we were made to find our life in God, to share in God's work of blessing others, and to find there a share in God's inexhaustible gladness?

9

The Church and Its Ministry:
Expanding an Ecumenical Vision

CHARLES M. WOOD

John Wesley has sometimes been called "a theologian of the Third Article," in view of the fact that the constant theme of most of his preaching and writing was the work of the Holy Spirit within creation and especially within those creatures who are being restored to their vocation "to know, to love, and to enjoy [their] Creator to all eternity."[1] Although the doctrine of the church is located prominently in the "third article" of the conventional creedal structure, Wesley had relatively little to say about the church. As is frequently observed, he had no intention of breaking with his own Church of England and thus no need to formulate an ecclesiology to justify such a move. Methodists did become a church, or churches, of course, "by a complicated process which it is partisan to defend and fruitless to deplore."[2] Methodist theologians of the nineteenth century on both sides of the Atlantic then produced some ecclesiological treatises, mainly in self-defense and mainly to insist that theirs was at least as truly a church as those of their detractors. These treatises, though, cannot be said to have had a profound influence on Methodist ecclesial self-consciousness.[3]

Fifty years ago, when the Oxford Institute of Methodist Theological Studies gathered to consider the theme of ecclesiology, Albert Outler posed the following question in his keynote address: "Do Methodists have

1. Wesley, "God's Approbation of His Works," 397.
2. Outler, "Do Methodists Have a Doctrine of the Church?," 19.
3. Representative might be Bangs, *An Original Church of Christ*.

a doctrine of the church?" His own answer was admittedly equivocal. He encouraged Wesley's theological heirs to recognize and own, for the time being, the amalgamated working doctrine of the church that was implicit in Wesleyan practice—but then, rather than worry much about a distinctively Methodist ecclesiology, to move forward along with other Christians toward "the *renewal* of catholicity" in the ecumenical quest for Christian unity. In the new configuration of a visibly unified church, Methodism might again function as Wesley intended it: not as a church in itself but "as a proper evangelical order of witness and worship, discipline and nurture."[4] Meanwhile, it was to the cause of Christian unity that Methodist efforts in ecclesiology should be directed.

When The United Methodist Church was formed in 1968 as a union between The Methodist Church and the Evangelical United Brethren Church, it appeared to have taken Outler's advice to heart. The preamble to the new body's constitution declares that "the Church of Jesus Christ exists in and for the world and its dividedness is a hindrance to its mission in that world." Article VI of that same constitution describes the new body as "part of the church universal," affirms as a common belief that "the Lord of the Church is calling Christians everywhere to strive toward unity," and commits The United Methodist Church to "seek, and work toward, unity at all levels of church life."[5] This ecumenical context and focus was in keeping with longstanding convictions and practices within the traditions that formed the new denomination. Accordingly, United Methodist theological reflection on the nature and mission of the church has been carried on primarily in the context of ecumenical encounter: in the various bilateral and multilateral dialogues, consultations, and Faith and Order discussions in which United Methodists along with representatives of the various other Methodist and Wesleyan communities have been regular participants.

The United Methodist Church was formed at a high point in ecumenical interest and apparent ecumenical progress. The Second Vatican Council (1962–65) had just concluded and its documents, including the landmark *Dogmatic Constitution on the Church* (*Lumen gentium*) and the *Decree on Ecumenism* (*Unitatis redintegratio*), were being received and welcomed by Christians of many traditions. Other promising ecumenical conversations and inter-church covenantal and union agreements were being pursued, both nationally and internationally. The Consultation on Church Union

4. Outler, "Do Methodists Have a Doctrine of the Church?," 27.

5. *Book of Discipline 2012*, 23, 25.

(COCU) in 1966 put forth a statement of "principles of church union" on which its participating denominations had achieved consensus, and it seemed to many leaders in these churches that actual visible unity was not too far away.[6] Many of those involved in (or simply observing) the process of this particular merger viewed it as a preliminary step toward a more comprehensive union just over the horizon. The same might be said, of course, regarding several other denominational mergers of the same era. At any rate, there is a deliberate provisionality pervading official United Methodist ecclesiology as it is expressed in the constitution and in subsequent church documents. It has made sense for United Methodist ecclesiological reflection to be devoted mainly to the wider endeavor of seeking a common understanding of the church with other Christians, rather than to the development of a distinctively United Methodist ecclesiology. Along the way, some of the persistent and pervasive characteristics of what one might call Methodist ecclesiality have become more clear, as they have been discovered (or have been pointed out) in the course of ecumenical encounters.

However, in recent years United Methodists along with many others have also experienced what some have called an "ecumenical winter." Formal dialogues continue at various levels and in some cases have achieved impressive results on paper, but they are marginal to the life of most churches. Many churches seem to have pulled back—if not in principle, at least in the actual investment of intellectual and other resources—from their commitments to the goal of visible Christian unity, or have recast those commitments in such a way as to call into question the extent of progress previously thought to have been made. The social changes, religious pluralism, and shifting religious demographics of a postmodern culture, both in the United States and around the globe, have given many religious traditions and communities acute concern about their own identity, survival, and well-being. Divisions *within* some of the churches on certain theological, ethical, and political issues seem to have overshadowed the divisions *among* the churches and to have diverted energy and attention inwards. In consequence, we have hardly begun to harvest the fruits of the ecumenical work in which we have been involved and to realize the contributions it can make to our self-understanding and practice.[7] Ironically, these neglected resources might well hold the key to the vision that is needed for our time. My aim here is to suggest how this is so.

6. Consultation on Church Union, *Principles of Church Union*.

7. Kasper, *Harvesting the Fruits*, esp. ch. 3.

In pursuing this aim, I will be appropriating to some modest degree what I take to be some Wesleyan contributions to ecclesiology, however implicit and indirect these may be. In the two most widely used Christian creeds (the Niceno-Constantinopolitan Creed and the Apostles' Creed), the subject that immediately follows the Holy Spirit in the third article is the church. Some commentators on these creeds have judged the immediate move from Spirit to church unfortunate, in that it may encourage the belief that the work of the Holy Spirit is confined to the church. The actual unfolding of the movement the Wesley brothers launched, however, when one takes into account the various branches of Methodist, Wesleyan, holiness, and Pentecostal Christianity, might lead one to just the opposite conclusion: that viewing the church in the context of the work of the Holy Spirit might lead to a more expansive, more challenging understanding of the church than our doctrines of the church have generally managed to convey.[8] Irenaeus of Lyon put the point succinctly and also radically when he wrote, "Where the church is, there also is the Spirit of God; and where the Spirit of God is, there is the church and all grace."[9] It is with the second half of that quotation that I am particularly occupied in what follows.

A recent article by a veteran participant-observer in ecumenical work, Michael Kinnamon, provides a convenient and useful summary of major points of agreement.[10] Kinnamon is both a leader and an interpreter of the ecumenical movement with experience in a variety of its forms, including some that have involved an unusually wide range of participant bodies. His article draws mainly on five texts produced under the auspices of the World Council of Churches, beginning with the Lima text of 1982, *Baptism, Eucharist and Ministry*, and ending with the draft version of the latest major document, *The Church*, which was considered by the Tenth Assembly of the World Council of Churches in Busan, South Korea, in the fall of 2013. At many places these texts embrace ecclesiological insights and affirmations enunciated in the major documents of the Second Vatican Council, which have enriched many of the numerous bilateral and multilateral

8. I am indebted to an unpublished address by William J. Abraham, "From the Linear to the Prototypical: An Ecclesiology of the Third Article," for some thoughts in this regard. He is not to be held responsible for the direction in which I have taken them.

9. Irenaeus, *Adversus Haereses* III, 24, 1, cited in Bobrinskoy, *Le mystère de l'Église*, 14.

10. Kinnamon, "What Can the Churches Say," 289–301. The article appears as chapter 4 in Kinnamon's 2014 book *Can a Renewal Movement Be Renewed? Questions for the Future of Ecumenism.*

conversations that have gone on over the past half-century.[11] In his article, Kinnamon offers "twelve points of growing agreement about the nature and purpose of the church."[12] He acknowledges that he might have had more, or fewer, points with a different arrangement of their substance. I will not offer a synopsis of the entire list here but will only mention some of the more salient areas of convergence and then identify some implications that I believe would require further development.

The point with which Kinnamon rightly begins is the common affirmation that the church is a gift of the triune God: "a gift of God, the creation of the Word of God and of the Holy Spirit."[13] What is meant by this is suggested in the wording of some contemporary eucharistic prayers, such as that currently in use in The United Methodist Church:

> Pour out your Holy Spirit on us, gathered here,
>   and on these gifts of bread and wine.
> Make them be for us the body and blood of Christ,
>   that we may be for the world the body of Christ,
>   redeemed by his blood.
> By your Spirit make us one with Christ,
>   one with each other,
>   and one in ministry to all the world . . .[14]

This is the point of the placement of the church in the third article of the Creed. By the Spirit the church is created, as human beings are incorporated into the sort of relationship with God and with one another that constitutes one sense of the term "the body of Christ." By the power of the Spirit, Christ is formed in them (Gal 4:19); in Christ, they are a new creation (2 Cor 5:17). The favored term for this relationship in the ecumenical thought of the last several decades is *koinonia*, communion or participation, a term whose New Testament usage immediately evokes associations with the Lord's Supper, the Holy Spirit, and the Holy Trinity (cf. 1 Cor 10:16; 2 Cor 13:14).

---

11. Anne Hunt has argued that "the most fundamental discovery" of Vatican II was "the church's origin in the mystery of the Trinity." As will be seen, this might be said to be the fundamental discovery at the heart of the developments Kinnamon is describing. Hunt, "Trinitarian Depths," 3.

12. Kinnamon, "What Can the Churches Say," 290.

13. Ibid., 292.

14. "A Service of Word and Table I," *United Methodist Hymnal*, 10.

A number of other affirmations follow closely upon this one, perhaps simply as implications that gradually emerge from this central insight. The church is "inherently one," as it is one body, one new humanity, into which its members are being formed. At the same time, its unity is "inherently diverse," given both the varieties and contingencies of human experience and the varieties of gifts of the one Spirit. The most apt vision for the character of Christian unity, then, is that of *koinonia* among diverse local churches or of "a communion of communions," as many Catholic documents and writers have expressed it. Each local community or manifestation of *koinonia* is itself enriched by the diversity within its membership—and diminished when that diversity is discouraged or suppressed. "What our texts suggest is that diversity is illegitimate when, and only when, it disrupts our communion and makes impossible the common confession of Jesus Christ as Lord and Savior."[15]

The comprehensive *koinonia* that is the church seeks and tends toward visible expression. The church, Kinnamon writes, can be thought of as both visible and invisible. There is "an invisible fellowship known only to God"—a fact that should keep Christians from claiming that their particular community simply is coextensive with the church—but at the same time the communion of the Holy Spirit drives toward tangible manifestation, embodiment.[16] There is remarkable consensus among the participants in the broad ecumenical discussion as to what this sort of visibility involves, and Kinnamon offers "a short list of 'tangible signs of the new life of communion'": shared confession of the apostolic faith, mutual recognition of members and ministries, shared celebration of the Eucharist, an ability to meet and make decisions together when appropriate, and cooperation in mission.[17]

In a later summary of these "fundamental bonds of communion," Kinnamon instances three of them—"common confession of faith, shared celebration of the Eucharist, common mission in the name of Christ"—in a way that suggests that this triad may be of particular importance.[18] It is, indeed, echoed in a point about converging understandings of a "representative ministry" in the church "that serves the unity of the church while also being a part of it." This ministry "builds up the body by preaching the

---

15. Kinnamon, "What Can the Churches Say," 294–95.
16. Ibid., 296.
17. Ibid. The internal quotation is from *Nature and Mission of the Church*, §32.
18. Kinnamon, "What Can the Churches Say," 297.

Word, celebrating the sacraments, and providing guidance in mission."[19] That this is not merely a triadic pattern but actually a trinitarian one (a further sign that the church's life as communion is "ultimately grounded in the communion of God the Holy Trinity"[20]) is a point to which we will return shortly.

I believe Kinnamon is correct in claiming that the extent of this convergence and the "thinking *together*" that has produced it amount to "a real breakthrough for the ecumenical movement, a significant contribution, not only to the search for Christian unity, but also to the renewal of existing churches, here and now."[21] I also believe that whether this potential is realized, or how soon, will depend in part upon whether and how readily three so far underdeveloped implications are given fuller attention. Each of these has to do, in its own way, with an issue that Kinnamon acknowledges as requiring further work: that of "the relationship between the institutional dimension of the church and the work of the Holy Spirit."[22]

The first has to do with the scope of the church itself or, one might say, with what we finally mean by "church." As Christopher Morse has observed, a great deal "depend[s] upon how the word *ekklēsia* is being defined."[23]

Kinnamon notes, as do the documents he is examining, that "church" has both a local and a universal reference: "the universal church is a communion of local churches, in each of which the fullness of the church resides. Each gathered community of believers, in which the gospel is preached and the sacraments are celebrated, in which Christ dwells by faith, is truly church—but not the whole of it."[24] This particular duality of reference— church as local, church as universal—goes back at least to Paul's usage of *ekklesia*. Another longstanding duality in the use of the term "church" has been eclipsed by the local/universal distinction in recent ecumenical discussion but may be very important to retrieve and re-employ. This is the distinction between the church as consisting of all who are being gathered into the people of God—all who are, or are being, saved—and the church as

---

19. Ibid.

20. Ibid., 295, quoting from the Porvoo Common Statement, §23.

21. Kinnamon, "What Can the Churches Say," 290.

22. Ibid., 300.

23. Morse, *Not Every Spirit*, 315. I have found the work of liturgical theologian Gordon W. Lathrop on the concept of *ekklesia* stimulating and fruitful. See Lathrop, *Holy People*, esp. ch. 3, and Lathrop and Wengert, *Christian Assembly*, ch 1.

24. Kinnamon, "What Can the Churches Say," 294.

a "sign and instrument" (to use the WCC language) of God's salvific work in the world. We might call the first of these senses of *ekklesia* the church as "community of salvation" and the second the church as "community of witness" or simply the "sign-community."[25]

One conventional way of making this distinction, of course, is as a distinction between the invisible and the visible church: a distinction attributable to Augustine but most commonly associated with the Protestant reformers, who incorporated it into the wording of confessions of faith as well as dogmatic treatises. Thus, the Westminster Confession of 1647—"the last major confessional statement of the Reformation"[26]—opens its chapter on the church with this very distinction:

> 1. The catholic or universal church, which is invisible, consists of the whole number of the elect, that have been, are, or shall be gathered into one, under Christ the Head thereof, and is the spouse, the body, the fullness of him that filleth all in all.

> 2. The visible church, which is also catholic or universal under the gospel (not confined to one nation as before under the law), consists of all those throughout the world that profess the true religion, and of their children, and is the kingdom of the Lord Jesus Christ, the house and family of God, out of which there is no ordinary possibility of salvation.[27]

The assumption generally made with this distinction in this form is that the invisible church, the community of salvation, is the smaller of the two bodies, and that its members (with a few exceptions) are or have been members of the visible church, the community of witness. Some professing or nominal Christians are "true Christians" but not all; and virtually all true Christians, in the sense of those who are saved through Christ, are also professing Christians. John Calvin's observation is typical:

> The Scriptures speak of the Church in two ways. Sometimes when they speak of the Church they mean the Church as it really is

25. I borrow these terms from Schubert M. Ogden, who is appropriating the concepts from Juan Luis Segundo, who is in turn building upon the work of Karl Rahner and of the Second Vatican Council. See for example Ogden, *Understanding of Christian Faith*, 95–107; Segundo, *The Community Called Church*; Rahner, *The Christian of the Future*.

26. Editors' introduction to the document, in Pelikan and Hotchkiss, *Creeds and Confessions*, 2:601.

27. Westminster Confession of Faith, ch. 25, in Pelikan and Hotchkiss, *Creeds and Confessions*, 2:638.

before God—the Church into which none are admitted but those who by the gift of adoption are sons of God, and by the sanctification of the Spirit true members of Christ. In this case it not only comprehends the saints who dwell on the earth, but all the elect who have existed from the beginning of the world. Often, too, by the name of Church is designated the whole body of mankind scattered throughout the world, who profess to worship one God and Christ, who by baptism are initiated into the faith; by partaking of the Lord's Supper profess unity in true doctrine and charity, agree in holding the word of the Lord, and observe the ministry which Christ has appointed for the preaching of it. In this Church there is a very large mixture of hypocrites, who have nothing of Christ but the name and outward appearance.[28]

An interesting thing has happened to this distinction in more recent years. For a number of reasons—including but not limited to our present understanding of the scope of human history and of human habitation of the planet—the notion that the possibility of salvation is "ordinarily" limited to professing Christians and probably to a small subset of those has seemed less tenable to many Christians. Needless to say, it does not seem so to all. A significant number of Christians and of church bodies continue to affirm a view along the lines of that of the Westminster Confession as commonly understood. Among the participant bodies in the ecumenical convergence summarized above, however, this is generally not the case.

In the latter half of the twentieth century, Karl Rahner became an influential representative of an alternative view. One element of this view makes explicit an implication of St. Cyprian's maxim that there is no salvation outside the church; namely, that if it is the case that human beings who are outside what the Westminster Confession calls the "visible church" can be saved, there must be, in some sense, *church* outside the church, that is, outside the "official" church, the body of professing or nominal Christians. This conviction concerning a broader scope of ecclesial existence than we may normally have in mind is not novel, nor is it unique to Rahner; it is found among notable figures in Christian antiquity and is shared by other contemporary theologians of various traditions. A second element in Rahner's view is perhaps more innovative: that is the suggestion that we would do well to acknowledge that this unofficial, off-the-grid mode of ecclesial existence may not be rare or exceptional but may instead be

28. Calvin, *Institutes*, 2:288 (IV, 1, 7).

the *ordinary* means of salvation and the ordinary form and experience of ecclesiality.[29]

Rahner did not adopt the terminology of visible and invisible church to express this distinction. That would have run counter to Catholic teaching since the Reformation, as well as counter to a sense that Rahner shared of the deep connection between (to use Irenaeus's language) "the church and all grace." Grace has an ecclesial tendency. It has to do with the creation and restoration of relationships, and those relationships, at least on the creaturely plane, are realized concretely. To speak, then, of church beyond the institutional church is not to speak of a set of individual human beings who happen in their individuality to be responding positively to God's offer of salvation. It is to speak of the way that the affirmative response to grace is leading them into genuine communion with the triune God and with fellow creatures, and thus into the one *ekklesia* even though in a non-explicit way. They are, Rahner would say, invisibly members of the one church, which is visible, and under the proper circumstances (i.e., if the opportunity were to become genuinely available), making that membership explicit would be the natural and desirable course.[30] In any event, for Rahner *ekklesia* in the sense of the community of salvation may vastly transcend *ekklesia* in the sense of the community that understands itself as sign and instrument of God's saving presence to the world. In view of the universal salvific will of God (1 Tim 2:4), Rahner believed, we are obliged to take this possibility seriously: we are "in duty bound hopefully to presume" that this is the case.[31] In keeping with this shift in perspective, Kinnamon observes that if the *koinonia* of which ecumenical documents speak is a "common partaking in the life of God, who as Trinity is the source and focus of communion," then it is much more than "a voluntary association of like-minded believers." "If the church is God's," Kinnamon writes, "then *we* don't set its boundaries or determine its entrance requirements."[32]

However, it is not clear to me that our ecumenical convergence to this point, as expressed in the documents Kinnamon discusses, has in fact taken this possibility with the seriousness it deserves. One might well come away

29. Rahner, *Church after the Council*, 53. For a recent critical assessment of Rahner's proposal, with fuller reference to the relevant sources, see Crowley, "Encountering the Religious Other," 567–85.

30. Rahner, *Theological Investigations*, 2:44–45.

31. Rahner, *Christian of the Future*, 86.

32. Kinnamon, "What Can the Churches Say," 292. The first quotation is a slightly modified passage from §13 of *The Nature and Mission of the Church*.

from a reading of this material with the impression that the judgment articulated by the Westminster assembly still stands: that outside the visibly constituted church "there is no ordinary possibility of salvation." Ecumenical experience may have led a number of church bodies to acknowledge more readily that the church is not coextensive with their own denomination or tradition and that there may be church, or at least elements of church, in Christian communities outside their own. Yet that the possibility of salvation outside the institutional church might entail that there is *church* outside the institutional church is a matter to which, it would seem from the content of these documents, those involved in ecumenical discussion have given little thought.

A second implication has to do with the character of that broader ecclesiality, and of its relationship to the specific ecclesiality of the church as community of witness. Because the church is a gift of the triune God, and in fact consists in a kind of participation in the life of the triune God, there is a triunity to be found throughout its own life. This is most clearly symbolized within the Christian community of witness by its representation of the threefold office of Christ. The Orthodox theologian and ecumenist Boris Bobrinskoy, in his systematic exposition of "the mystery of the church," writes of "the threefold ministry of the church" in such a way as to show the correspondences to Christ's priestly, royal, and prophetic offices of the priestly, royal, and prophetic ministry of the whole church.[33] In its account of the laity (par. 31), the *Dogmatic Constitution on the Church* describes the laity as "all the faithful . . . who by baptism are incorporated into Christ, are constituted the people of God, who have been made sharers in their own way in the priestly, prophetic, and kingly office of Christ and play their part in carrying out the mission of the whole Christian people in the church and in the world."[34] This understanding of the threefold ministry of the whole people of God has not been as strongly affirmed among Protestants, at least in this way, though it has a parallel in many Protestant explications of the "marks of the church" and can be traced in occasional ecumenical statements.[35] For example, the International Methodist-Catholic Dialogue

33. Bobrinskoy, *Le mystère de l'Église*, 6.

34. Fannery, *Vatican Council II*, 48-49.

35. The report of the first North American Conference on Faith and Order (Oberlin, 1957) characterizes the "apostolic task" of the churches as "to witness to the Gospel and to bring its redeeming power to bear upon every aspect of human life. For this task it has been given an ordered life of Word, sacraments and ministry which is to be exercised in and by the power of the Holy Spirit" (Minear, *Nature of the Unity We Seek*, 206).

Commission could affirm in its Brighton Report (2001), "Because Christ's followers are incorporated into him through baptism, they share in his priestly, prophetic and royal office, together as a communion and individually each in their own way."[36] *Lumen gentium* applies the same three-aspect structure to its discussion of the tasks of each of the ordained ministries, in a pattern that is also historically common in other traditions and that has become familiar in the more recent ecumenical discussion from *Baptism, Eucharist, and Ministry*: "The chief responsibility of the ordained ministry is to assemble and build up the body of Christ by proclaiming and teaching the Word of God, by celebrating the sacraments, and by guiding the life of the community in its worship, its mission and its caring ministry."[37]

This triune pattern, however, should not be limited in its scope to the Christian community of witness. It belongs to what Rahner would regard as the broader *ekklesia*, the "community of salvation" as such, precisely because of the nature of the *koinonia* that salvation brings.

John Wesley urged the early Methodists to proclaim Christ "in all his offices."[38] We have already seen that for Wesley, as for substantial parts of Christian tradition, to be created in the image of God is to be "designed to know, to love, and to enjoy [our] Creator to all eternity."[39] His interpretation of the "fall" involved an account of the human loss of those capacities for knowledge, love, and joy; and his soteriology was all about their recovery: our renewal in the image of God. (It is a triune image, *imago Trinitatis*;

36. "Speaking the Truth in Love," §§35–36, cited in Putney and Wainwright, "Synthesis," §73.

37. World Council of Churches, *Baptism, Eucharist and Ministry*, 22 ("Ministry," II, 13). See Borght, *Theology of Ministry*, for an acute and insightful historical and theological treatment of this theme.

38. Wesley declares, "We are not ourselves clear before God, unless we proclaim him in all his offices. To preach Christ, as a workman that needeth not to be ashamed, is to preach him, not only as our great High Priest, 'taken from among men, and ordained for men, in things pertaining to God;' as such, 'reconciling us to God by his blood,' and 'ever living to make intercession for us;'—but likewise as the Prophet of the Lord, 'who of God is made unto us wisdom,' who, by his word and his Spirit, is with us always, 'guiding us into all truth;'—yea, and as remaining a King for ever; as giving laws to all whom he has bought with his blood; as restoring those to the image of God, whom he had first reinstated in his favour; as reigning in all believing hearts until he has 'subdued all things to himself,'—until he hath utterly cast out all sin, and brought in everlasting righteousness" ("The Law Established through Faith, Discourse II," I.6, in *Works* [Outler], 2:37–38). A further short exposition of the three offices (and our need of them) is to be found in Wesley's note on Matt 1:16 in his *Explanatory Notes Upon the New Testament*.

39. Wesley, "God's Approbation of His Works," 397.

we are, in a line from Charles Wesley, "ordained to be / transcripts of the Trinity."[40]) The threefold office of Christ addresses all three aspects of the human vocation and of the sin that has distorted them. Wesley wanted the Methodists to keep that comprehensive vision in mind and not to settle for reductionistic accounts of salvation—"one-office" accounts, as often prevailed in earlier ages and into his own time and ours.

Salvation is, as Wesley put it, "a present thing," encompassing "the entire work of God, from the first dawning of grace in the soul till it is consummated in glory."[41] The transformation of human lives grounded in the work of Christ and appropriated in the power of the Holy Spirit amounts to a recovery of the human vocation to glorify God in knowledge, joy, and love. It is a recovery "in part" under present conditions, but it is a real recovery. Doctrines of sanctification in all their variety (and with such convergences as are represented by the *Joint Declaration on the Doctrine of Justification* and its ongoing ecumenical reception) are attempts to honor that fact. If the fruit of justification is "a Christian life lived in faith, hope, and love,"[42] then something quite analogous to those "Christian" virtues must also characterize the lives of all who are being saved, whatever their explicit relation (or lack of one) to the Christian community of witness. That latter community with its ministry of Word, Sacrament, and Order is to serve as a sign and instrument of the broader *ekklesia* that God is bringing forth. We would do well to be attentive to the evidence of that new creation, wherever it is coming to be.

This brings me to the third implication to be pursued, which I can do little more than mention here. It has to do both with the "sign and instrument" function of the community of witness and with the question of attentiveness to evidence of the *ekklesia* beyond that community's boundaries.

Some of the limitations of the traditional distinction between a visible and an invisible church have been noted, but there is a passage in the Westminster Confession utilizing that distinction in a way that might provide some help in this connection. "This catholic church," it reads, "hath been sometimes more, sometimes less visible. And particular churches, which are members thereof, are more or less pure, according as the doctrine of

40. "Sinners, Turn: Why Will You Die?," *United Methodist Hymnal,* #346.
41. Wesley, "Scripture Way of Salvation," 156.
42. *Joint Declaration on the Doctrine of Justification,* 24 (§37).

the gospel is taught and embraced, ordinances administered, and public worship performed more or less purely in them."[43]

The original intent of this passage may well have been polemical, but a more self-critical as well as a more constructive usage might be commended. What is immediately striking is that the "visibility" of the church here is not equated with what is empirically evident or with institutional reality. The visibility of a church does not necessarily increase or diminish with its real estate holdings, budget, membership, brand recognition, or other standard markers of success. Its visibility is of a different order: To what extent is the gospel taught and embraced? To what extent can it be said that the God of Jesus Christ is known and worshiped? To what extent does this community live by and manifest "the grace of our Lord Jesus Christ, and the love of God, and the communion of the Holy Spirit" (2 Cor 13:14)? What in the character of this community's life and witness seems to inhibit or threaten, rather than foster, the glorification of God through knowledge, love, and joy?

What questions should be asked along these lines, and how to pursue them, are obviously matters that require some reflection. The acknowledgment that the church is a "church of sinners" is fairly common in churchly and ecumenical statements, but by itself this does not yet get us very far. Studies of what might be called "the human uses of the church"—its political, social, psychological, "religious," and cultural uses, for instance—are what is required if our theological understanding of the church is not to remain unhelpfully abstract and remote from actuality. There have been times over the past several decades when the ecclesiological pertinence of such inquiries has been recognized and times when they have tended to fall by the wayside, even when they have been conducted under ecumenical auspices. The issues they raise and the facts they bring to our attention are often matters of some sensitivity in an ecumenical forum or, for that matter, within many of the churches—which may be one reason they have not yet received there the fuller reception and use that they urgently require.

As a counterpart to this exercise in self-criticism, those who are members of the Christian community of witness might raise a different set of questions for the sake of a proper attentiveness to the *ekklesia* beyond its boundaries. Where and how might "the grace of our Lord Jesus Christ, and the love of God, and the communion of the Holy Spirit" be discerned among

43. Westminster Confession of Faith, 25.4, in Pelikan and Hotchkiss, *Creeds and Confessions*, 2:639.

people who do not identify themselves as Christians? How, in other words, might the *ekklesia* be finding a kind of visibility beyond the Christian community of witness? Scholars pursuing several contemporary theological inquiries involving relationships between Christianity and other religious traditions are among those who might have much to offer to constructive ecumenical ecclesiology in this regard, though to limit the range of investigation to the "religious other" would be unwise.

I must acknowledge that all three of the points I have introduced here concerning what Michael Kinnamon calls "the relationship between the institutional dimension of the church and the work of the Holy Spirit" may in fact not be points of emerging consensus ripe for development but rather points of contention. The reason they have not been explored further in an ecumenical context is precisely that. Nevertheless, I suspect that a constructive ecclesiological vision that tried to reckon more fully with them would be a worthwhile endeavor.

Bibliography

Bangs, Nathan. *An Original Church of Christ, or Scriptural Vindication of the Orders and Powers of the Ministry of the Methodist Episcopal Church.* New York: T. Mason and G. Lane, 1837.

Bobrinskoy, Boris. *Le mystère de l'Église: Cours de théologie dogmatique.* Paris: Cerf, 2003.

The Book of Discipline of The United Methodist Church 2012. Nashville: United Methodist Publishing House, 2012.

Borght, Ed. A. J. G. van der. *Theology of Ministry: A Reformed Contribution to an Ecumenical Dialogue.* Leiden: Brill, 2007.

Calvin, John. *Institutes of the Christian Religion.* Translated by Henry Beveridge. Vol. 2. London: James Clarke, 1962.

Crowley, Paul G. "Encountering the Religious Other: Challenges to Rahner's Transcendental Project." *Theological Studies* 71 (2010) 567–85.

Consultation on Church Union. *Principles of Church Union; Adopted by the Consultation at Its Meeting 1966.* Cincinnati: Forward Movement, 1966.

Flannery, Austin, ed. *Vatican Council II: The Basic Sixteen Documents; Constitutions, Decrees, Declarations.* Northport, NY: Costello, 1996.

Hunt, Anne. "The Trinitarian Depths of Vatican II." *Theological Studies* 74 (2013) 3–19.

Kasper, Cardinal Walter. *Harvesting the Fruits: Basic Aspects of Christian Faith in Ecumenical Dialogue.* New York: Continuum, 2009.

Kinnamon, Michael. "What Can the Churches Say Together about the Church?" *Ecclesiology* 8 (2012) 289–301.

Lathrop, Gordon W. *Holy People: A Liturgical Ecclesiology.* Minneapolis: Fortress, 1999.

Lathrop, Gordon W., and Timothy J. Wengert. *Christian Assembly: Marks of the Church in a Pluralistic Age.* Minneapolis: Fortress, 2004.

The Lutheran World Federation and the Roman Catholic Church. *Joint Declaration on the Doctrine of Justification*. Grand Rapids: Eerdmans, 2000.

Minear, Paul S., ed. *The Nature of the Unity We Seek*. St. Louis: Bethany, 1958.

Morse, Christopher. *Not Every Spirit: A Dogmatics of Christian Disbelief*. 2nd ed. New York: Continuum, 2009.

Ogden, Schubert M. *The Understanding of Christian Faith*. Eugene, OR: Cascade, 2010.

Outler, Albert C. "Do Methodists Have a Doctrine of the Church?" In *The Doctrine of the Church*, edited by Dow Kirkpatrick, 11–28. Nashville: Abingdon, 1964.

Pelikan, Jaroslav, and Valerie Hotchkiss, eds. *Creeds and Confessions of Faith in the Christian Tradition*. Vol. 2. New Haven: Yale University Press, 2003.

Putney, Michael E., and Geoffrey Wainwright. "Synthesis: Together to Holiness; Forty Years of Methodist and Roman Catholic Dialogue." http://worldmethodistcouncil. org/wp-content/uploads/2012/02/Roman-Catholic-Dialogue-Synthesis-Report.pdf.

Rahner, Karl. *Theological Investigations*. Vol. 2, *Man in the Church*. Baltimore: Helicon, 1963.

———. *The Christian of the Future*. Translated by W. J. O'Hara. New York: Herder & Herder, 1967.

———. *The Church after the Council*. Translated by D. C. Herron and R. Albrecht. New York: Herder & Herder, 1966.

Segundo, Juan Luis. *The Community Called Church*. Maryknoll, NY: Orbis, 1973.

The United Methodist Hymnal. Nashville: United Methodist Publishing House, 1989.

Wesley, John. "God's Approbation of His Works." In vol. 2 of *The Works of John Wesley*, edited by Albert C. Outler. Nashville: Abingdon, 1985.

———. "The Scripture Way of Salvation." In vol. 2 *The Works of John Wesley*, edited by Albert C. Outler. Nashville: Abingdon, 1985.

World Council of Churches. *Baptism, Eucharist and Ministry*. Faith and Order Paper No. 111. Geneva: World Council of Churches, 1982.

10

Who Hopes for What He Already Sees?

JOSIAH U. YOUNG III

During a committee meeting at Wesley Theological Seminary, I said something like "caste privilege is here to stay." Doug Meeks, then the academic dean of the seminary and chair of the committee, said immediately, "You don't know that." I had no comeback, because he was absolutely right. I did not know that. What I said, moreover, did not reflect what I hoped for, either then or now. It was good to be reminded that cynicism has no place in Christian spirituality. In this essay, I will discuss some of the implications of this spirituality. I will focus, first, on some of its biblical foundations. Second, I will discuss excerpts from two of Doug Meeks's books, *Origins of the Theology of Hope* and *God the Economist*, that are pertinent to the biblical passages I will highlight. Third, I will offer a few concluding reflections on what I do know about hope.

Apocalyptic Promises

Reframing the words of nineteenth-century abolitionist Theodore Parker, Martin Luther King Jr. often said that "the arc of the moral universe is long, but it bends toward justice."[1] In writing this essay, it dawned on me that the rainbow of Gen 9:13 can be construed as God's promise to bend the moral universe in heaven toward justice on earth. The rainbow is a cosmic sign of a vow God made to himself after he had plunged most of his creation back

---

1. Branch, *Parting the Waters*, 197.

124

into the void. The Lord had let the primal waters loose: "all the fountains of the great deep burst forth, and the windows of the heavens were opened." He flooded the earth: "all the high mountains under the whole heaven were covered." Only Noah and those who belonged to him were left alive (Gen 7:13–16). When God shut off the water and the land was finally dry enough to walk on, Noah built an Abel-like altar to the Lord. The offering of flesh transformed into spirit, so to speak, moved the Lord; for God "smelled the pleasing odor," and said "in his heart,"

> I will never again curse the ground because of humankind, for the inclination of the human heart is evil from youth; nor will I ever again destroy every living creature as I have done. As long as the earth endures, seedtime and harvest, cold and heat, summer and winter, day and night, shall not cease. (Gen 8:21–22)

And since Noah was a righteous person, God made a covenant with him:

> I have set my bow in the clouds, and it shall be a sign of the covenant between me and the earth. When I bring clouds over the earth and the bow is seen in the clouds, I will remember my covenant that is between me and you and every living creature of all flesh; and the waters shall never again become a flood to destroy all flesh. (Gen 9:13–16)

One can say that God and his only-begotten Son remember Noah's sacrifice well on Golgotha as they suffer the post-flood promise there, evincing that what the elders say is true: "God is good all the time." Moreover, God made his promise good when he raised the Christ, his image (Gen 1:26), from the void. God's Word is his bond, his righteousness, his justice. Although sinners crucified Christ because "the inclination of the human heart is evil from youth," the risen Christ is, as it were, the rainbow sign in Spirit and in truth. Those who believe in the resurrection and the life know that God keeps his Word. One feels certain about it. One does not feel that one is betting on something that might not pan out, for hope is the certainty that we will not perish. Christ has given those who believe in him the assurance that everything will be all right (John 20:22; Acts 2:2). As Paul has put it, hope is "laid up for you in heaven" (Col 1:5). Heaven, the created "sphere of God's creative potentialities and energies," is the place from which God sends the Holy Spirit through the ascended Christ.[2] To

2. Moltmann, *God in Creation*, 182.

quote Titus 3:6–8, God has poured out the Holy Spirit "richly through Jesus Christ our Savior, so that, having been justified by his grace, we might
become heirs according to the hope of eternal life. The saying is sure." (See
also Acts 1:5–11 and 2:1–4.) In the Spirit, hope—the *mysterion*—is "Christ
in you" (Col 1:27). "I'm so glad trouble don't last always," the old song says,
because "the future," as Doug Meeks has put it, "is the 'power of God' to
realize his righteousness in everything that is."[3] Who among the children of
God has time for negative thinking? The world God has created is here to
stay, and it will be redeemed. Not in its present form. Not without changing. Yet I suspect that it will endure with great continuity. God deemed
the creation to be very good from the time he shed light on it (Gen 1:4).
Why would he take away the creation's solidity and height and breadth and
scope? Not even the flood annihilated them.

According to New Testament scholar N. T. Wright, first-century Christians such as Paul "were not hoping to escape from the present universe into
some Platonic realm of eternal bliss enjoyed by disembodied souls after the
end of the space-time universe." Rather, those who upheld the resurrection
hoped to be restored as new creations—as "new bodies" (spiritual ones,
according to Paul)—so that they would be able to revel in "the very much
this-worldly shalom, peace and prosperity that was in store."[4] Paul writes,
"For the creation was subjected to futility, not of its own will but by the will
of the one who subjected it, in hope that the creation itself will be set free
from its bondage to decay and will obtain the freedom of the glory of the
children of God" (Rom 8:20–21). It seems to me that hope in this sense is
not a potentiality but an actuality in the risen and ascended Lord.

The second-century text 3 Baruch (the Greek Apocalypse of Baruch)
seems to corroborate Paul's witness. Here, one of God's angels takes Baruch
up into the heavens where he learns secrets of the fall and the flood. Heaven
unveils that a fallen angel plants a nasty vine near the tree of knowledge to
corrupt Paradise. God curses the vine, which had wrapped itself around the
tree, and forbids Adam to go near it. Adam disobeys and brings sin into the
world. After the flood, Noah finds fragments of the poison vine and ago-
nizes about what to do with them. God instructs Noah to plant the traces
of the vine (presumably because the Lord had vowed to make the best of
what he had made to actualize the future he has in store for the creation):

---

3. Meeks, *Origins of Hope*, 86.
4. Wright, *New Testament and the People of God*, 286.

> God sent his angel Sarasael, and said, "Arise, Noah, and plant the
> shoot of the vine, for thus says the Lord: 'Its bitterness will be
> changed into sweetness, and its curse will become a blessing, and
> that which is produced from it will become the blood of God; and
> as through it the human race obtained condemnation, so again
> through Jesus Christ the Immanuel will they receive in Him the
> upward calling, and the entry into paradise.'" (3 Bar 4:15)[5]

The antibody to death is found in the vine God has transformed, in Christ.
He is "the true vine," and his "Father is the vinegrower. He removes every
branch in me that bears no fruit. Every branch that bears fruit he prunes to
make it bear more fruit" (John 15:1–2).

Another extracanonical text roughly contemporaneous with Paul's
time also corroborates his testimony in outing the future's actuality force-
fully. The Apocalypse of Abraham dates from the Roman destruction of the
temple and recounts a *mysterion*: an angel promises to show Abraham what
"is in the heavens, on the earth and in the sea, in the abyss, and in the lower
depths, in the garden of Eden and in its rivers, in the fullness of the universe." On angel's wings, Abraham will see creation's "circles in all."[6] What
Abraham will see, N. T. Wright argues, constitutes the essence of apocalyptic: God unveils all kinds of secrets to Abraham. "As a result he learns new
ways of worshipping" the Creator.[7] Abraham learns—to put it heuristically
in the words of Henrich Heine—that "everything is not God," but "God is
everything."[8] The heavens, the earth, and the deep attest to their Creator
in their own ways and in varying degrees. And when God unveils their
meaning, they bear witness to the rainbow sign. For God's Spirit "circles in
all creation" as he molds the cosmos into "a dynamic web of interconnected
processes . . . open for God and for his future," as Jürgen Moltmann put it.[9]
Moltmann suggests, in addition, that immortals such as Sarasael prefigure
the reality "of eternal life" in "the modality of . . . the resurrection."[10] As Paul
put it in Rom 1:20, the Creator's "eternal power and divine nature, invisible
though they are," were present from day one of the creation and "have been
understood and seen through the things he has made."

5. See http://www.pseudepigrapha.com/pseudepigrapha/3Baruch.html.

6. *Apoc. Ab.* 12.9–10, as quoted in Wright, *New Testament and the People of God*, 281.

7. Wright, *New Testament and the People of God*, 281.

8. As quoted in Moltmann, *God in Creation*, 103.

9. Ibid.

10. Ibid., 184.

God's power is so great, Paul avows, that "those who are in Christ Jesus" need not attempt to fulfill the Mosaic law. This is because "the law of the Spirit of life" has set them "free from the law of sin and of death" (Rom 8:2). The law of the Spirit of life invigorates life here and now as it makes even toxic things toxoids for us and for our salvation (as 3 Baruch has pointed out). One cannot corrupt the law of the Spirit of life; "for God," Paul writes, "has done what the law, weakened by the flesh, could not do: by sending his own Son in the likeness of sinful flesh, and to deal with sin, he condemned sin in the flesh, so that the just requirement of the law might be fulfilled in us, who walk not according to the flesh but according to the Spirit" (Rom 8:3–4). The Holy Spirit empowers us to look on the rainbow side (Easter) and eschew cynicism ("things will never change") as blasphemous. Cynicism—the view that evil will prevail—promotes sin as the cynical surrender (sometimes unwittingly) to the hegemony of the principalities and powers that displease God. If one says in one's heart "injustice is permanent," he or she strengthens injustice because even the slight acquiescence in wickedness empowers it. If injustice is permanent, why fight it? Such resignation is "flesh."

As Paul put it in Rom 8:5–8,

> Those who live according to the flesh set their minds on the things of the flesh, but those who live according to the Spirit set their minds on the things of the Spirit. To set the mind on the flesh is death, but to set the mind on the Spirit is life and peace. For this reason the mind that is set on the flesh is hostile to God; it does not submit to God's law—indeed it cannot, and those who are in the flesh cannot please God.

Doug Meeks brings out some of the contemporary implications of Paul's flesh-Spirit dialectic in writing of "God's law" as the antidote to our problematic global economy.

Beyond Promethean Presumption and Sisyphean Despair[11]

Doug Meeks argues compellingly that the current state of the world's political economy does not please God because these structures deprive millions of poor and oppressed people around the world of fullness of life. At present, the global market values wealth and prosperity for a few. According

11. Meeks, *Origins of Hope*, 4.

to Meeks, these values blatantly disregard biblical faith. "It is not only that God is not desired," Meeks asserts, "God is also not needed in the modern market." The modern market surely has its "God concepts," however—whatever makes up one's heart's desire may be said to be "god" for that person.[12] Unbridled profit and uncommon luxury, therefore, signify "god" for those whose ultimate concern is nothing but the market such as it is. Meeks argues, "within the market itself it is unwise, if not impossible" to grant entrance to God in Christ.[13] According to Meeks,

> Presidents may refer to God in political addresses as an element of the control functions of politics. But in their peculiarly economic activity, their corporation executives, economists, and consumers at the local hardware store do not think to call on God for any conceivable purpose, however religious they perceive themselves to be.[14]

For Meeks, however, Christ's Father unveils in his Son what he intends the world to be—a household (*oikonomia tou theou*), in which the world's resources will be justly distributed and free of domination by inhumane empires. For Meeks, moreover, it is apostasy for the church not to work for the *oikonomia tou theou* at present.

According to Doug Meeks, a church that models God's household embodies "the dialectic of reconciliation"—"the thorough interdependence" of those whom God has called to be Christians and the contemporary "relevance" of that call. The tension between call and relevance provokes Christians to name and resist what displeases the Holy Spirit here and now.[15] Meeks is of the view, in addition, that Christians cannot name and resist Godlessness if they seek refuge in symbols that can prevent movement toward God's future.[16] Yesterday's ancient theologies are surely edifying, but they are not necessarily helpful to down-and-out people today.

Service to the world's mistreated people often brings suffering because those who seem to run the world are not above punishing those who

---

12. Feuerbach, *Essence of Christianity*, 10–11. "Whatever is God to a man, that is his heart and soul; and conversely, God is the manifested inward nature, the expressed self of a man—religion the solemn unveiling of a man's hidden treasures, the revelation of his intimate thoughts, the open confession of his love-secrets."

13. Meeks, *God the Economist*, 47.

14. Ibid.

15. Meeks, *Origins of Hope*, 3.

16. Ibid., 2.

endanger wealth and privilege. The Hellenistic notion that God is incapable of suffering and so indifferent to worldly contradictions is often helpful to the wealthy and privileged because such a notion removes God from conflict. The fact that the few are opulently set for life whereas the majority barely get by would not be a theological problem. In fact, the notion that God is essentially impassible may invite indifference to some of our most difficult problems today. But do the ancient contradictions that are part of Christ's Golgotha experience have nothing to do with today? Is the fact that Christ's death stemmed from his obedience to Israel's God not a theological matter for today? Was his faithfulness to Noah's and Abraham's God of no consequence to God?

One can surely attribute Christ's *Eloi, Eloi, lema sabachthani?* cry to a nonpersonal human nature so that the immutability of the "One" remains sacrosanct. But one gets the impression from the scriptures that such a substance (*homoousios* with the Father) may have little to do with the Lord whom Noah's altar moved so intensely. The *lema sabachthani* cry is certainly peculiar to the Son, and yet one deduces that his cry unveils the anguish of the Father too, for the Lord is joined to Israel's messiah at the hip (Hos 11:1; Matt 2:15). The two are in one another through the Spirit.[17] Through the Spirit, Meeks writes, the "Father gives away the Son," and through the Spirit, "the Son gives away himself; both go outside themselves and both suffer."[18] Both are so open to the world that they are mortified by the collusion between Rome and the temple priesthood. By way of his *pneumatologia crucis*, Doug Meeks thus criticizes all notions that God is a "self-sufficient and passionless" monad. For Meeks, moreover, the Holy Spirit—the law of life—is the suffering God's Advocate. The Spirit makes present "God's righteousness . . . God's power for life against death," for Christ's sake.[19]

Does God's righteousness have no bearing on the injustices that trouble the masses today? The answer is surely yes if Christians acquiesce in the status quo simply to get along in it. Oftentimes, resistance to the status quo is painful. Pain can depress one and lead one to give up. Then too, one can fool oneself into thinking that action against the status quo will bring about quick, utopian results. (Some of us formed by the 1960s civil rights and Black Power movements thought the ghetto would soon become

17. See Moltmann, *The Trinity and the Kingdom.*

18. Meeks, *God the Economist,* 170.

19. Ibid., 170–71.

a Shangri-La thanks to fire that raged in our souls. We were wrong.[20])
Those in the Spirit know, however, that resistance does not spring from
Promethean presumption or Sisyphean despair. Both "simply ride the ups
and downs of history" without hope. Hope, however, "is mediated through
the text of hope."[21]

As Romans 8, the aforementioned apocryphal texts, and Genesis 9
point out, hope texts unveil that no ideology can marginalize others in God's
household *ad infinitum*—all will "get what it takes to live." To knit Meeks
and Paul together, the law of the Spirit of life will distribute the wealth so
that all people might attain a "livelihood," the "symbiosis with nature, and
see the world as a mutually recognized and supportive habitat in peace."[22]
The futurity of this hope sits at God's right hand and fills the depths and
the heights of the cosmos presently in the Spirit, who proceeds from the
Father of the Son (John 15:26). Anyone who assumes that things will not
change, that the injustice rampant today will be rampant tomorrow, are
"in the flesh" and "cannot please God" (Rom 8:8). Flesh is therefore to the
history that is passing away as the Spirit of Christ is to the righteous history
that we make with God's help. With the Spirit's counsel, we make history as
"the history of the future."[23] Led "by the Spirit of God" as "children of God,"
we are marching toward tomorrow in faith and hope. We have not received
"a spirit of slavery to fall back into fear, but . . . a spirit of adoption." According to Paul, every time we shout "Father-God," the Holy Spirit is "bearing
witness with our spirit that we are children of God." As children of God, we
are "heirs of God and joint heirs with Christ—if, in fact, we suffer with him
so that we may also be glorified with him." For Paul, moreover, "the sufferings of this present time are not worth comparing with the glory about to
be revealed to us" (Rom 8:18).

Hoping for What One Does Not See

I have seen the misery of this present time with my own eyes in my own
country, but rarely have I seen that misery match the wretchedness I have
witnessed in other countries. The Democratic Republic of Congo (DRC),
which I visited in 2011, comes to mind. There is virtually no infrastructure

20. See Alexander, *The New Jim Crow: Mass Incarceration in the Age of Colorblindness.*

21. Meeks, *Origins of Hope,* 7.

22. Meeks, *God the Economist,* 34.

23. See Moltmann, *Way of Jesus Christ,* 234–35.

to speak of, armed soldiers are staked out everywhere, and the indigence of the people is staggering.[24] Most of the people whom I observed in Kinshasa, the capital city, seemed frantically in search of their daily bread. I saw young boys straining under loads of burlap bags filled with manioc flour. Ashy from the white cassava dust, they trudged miserably about Kinshasa. An armed guard accompanying me and my compatriots took us to a fishing village so that we could get a good look at the powerful, legendary Congo River. As we walked on the sandy road toward the river, a young peasant woman with a large bowl on her head approached me. Most people with bundles on their heads walked with their arms at their sides, but this woman kept one hand on top of the bowl she carried. She took the bowl from her head and took off its top while speaking in a tongue unknown to me. Locusts swarmed within the bowl. I don't know why she singled me out for these treats. Maybe she thought I could afford them. I do know that selling insects is a hard way to make a living.

In his book *God the Economist*, Doug Meeks argues that work must be redeemed. According to Meeks, God intended humankind to work contentedly and productively; but humankind chose the unrighteous path. The root of this unrighteousness is Adam's fall, which flowered in the primal fratricide (Gen 4:8). Subsequently, work has meant "'no freedom' . . . one's labor is expropriated by another. One plants and another harvests. One builds and another occupies."[25] Sin of this kind is structural: "The very power God gives for work is also the power by which human beings set themselves over against God, destroy creation, and turn the human community into constant strife, fear, and anxious greed."[26] As I see it, the locust woman's drudgery is a consequence of the structural sin Meeks discusses in *God the Economist*. I do not mean that the locust woman deserves her fate

24. The DRC is still reeling from what scholars call Africa's World War, which escalated in the aftermath of the Rwandan holocaust (1994). The Tutsi army that ended the genocide sought to bring the Hutu *génocidaires* to justice. President Mobutu had given them sanctuary in eastern Congo and armed them to help them overthrow the new Tutsi-run regime in Rwanda. Mobutu's gross exploitation of his people for personal gain, however, made him vulnerable to Congolese insurgent Laurent Kabila, who finally toppled Mobutu with the help of Rwandan general Paul Kagame's crackerjack Tutsi-dominated army and his allies—Uganda, Zimbabwe, Kenya, Tanzania, and Angola. The Kabila-run government ended, however, with Kabila's assassination by one of his own men, thus plunging the Congolese people into another long stretch of violence and mass death. A reported three million Africans had died by 2005, most of them from starvation!

25. Meeks, *God the Economist*, 146.

26. Ibid.

because of her sinfulness. I don't find anything wrong with her selling the delicacies—if that is what they were (Acts 10)! It is rather the case that the sin that enslaves her has to do with the precolonial, colonial, and neocolonial history of the Congo.[27]

Meeks points out that "Israel's history with God begins with the stark reality of human bondage through forced labor."[28] YHWH surely reveals himself to Shem's progeny by liberating them from the Egyptians after slaying their firstborn (Ham's progeny). God's faithfulness to the Noachic covenant is thus borne out in his liberation of "Shem," Abraham's ancestor. God's rainbow sign is made good in Shem's liberation. One cannot avoid the troubling conclusion, moreover, that Israel enslaved some of Ham's descendants (Lev 25).[29] The fact that God's word sanctioned the enslavement of non-Hebrew people is troubling. Meeks points out that King Solomon "builds the house of the Lord with the *corvée*, 'forced labor' (1 Kings 9:15)." He argues that Solomon's ruthlessness in that regard is abominable: "No one may 'own' the labor of another person."[30] If that is true—and it surely is for me—what is one to make of Lev 25:44–46? Shouldn't the jubilee be for all?

One can only hope that Paul's mission to the Gentiles has laid the enmity among Noah's progeny to rest for Christ's sake. For isn't it true that the Easter event reveals more so than any other biblical happening that God does not intend for his creation to toil in the heat until death? For the vow God made to preserve and redeem the creation was kept, Meeks writes, through the sacrifice that liberates "*everything that is* out of the chaos of nothingness."[31] God made the sacrifice Abraham did not have to make. "Through the sacrifice of the Son, God takes into God's own community

---

27. See Young, *The African Colonial State*.

28. Meeks, *God the Economist*, 146.

29. "As for the male and female slaves whom you may have, it is from the nations around you that you may acquire male and female slaves. You may also acquire them from among the aliens residing with you, and from their families that are with you, who have been born in your land; and they may be your property. You may keep them as a possession for your children after you, for them to inherit as property. These you may treat as slaves, but as for your fellow Israelites, no one shall rule over the other with harshness" (Lev 25:44–46). Apparently, YHWH's love of freedom extended only so far at that time.

30. Meeks, *God the Economist*, 147.

31. Ibid., 148, emphasis added.

the human death-serving work which is sin. This is God's grief work."[32] It is, apparently, the only work that brings about the future—a time when people such as the poor, war-torn and oppressed Congolese will enjoy the resources of the wide, fertile space God has placed them in. How *passé* my concern about caste privilege will be then!

I probably will not live long enough to see that future. I don't know that; but why should I be different from the countless others who hoped for what they did not get to see? I am not cynical, though. I am hopeful. The "Spirit helps us in our weakness"; even when "we do not know how to pray as we ought," Paul writes, "that very Spirit intercedes with sighs too deep for words. And God, who searches the heart, knows what is the mind of the Spirit, because the Spirit intercedes for the saints according to the will of God" (Rom 8:26–27). What is more: "If God is for us, who is against us? He who did not withhold his own Son, but gave him up for all of us, will he not with him also give us everything else? . . . Who will separate us from the love of Christ? Will hardship, or distress, or persecution, or famine, or nakedness, or peril, or sword? . . . For I am convinced that neither death, nor life, nor angels, nor rulers, nor things present, nor things to come, nor powers, nor height, nor depth, nor anything else in all creation, will be able to separate us from the love of God in Christ Jesus our Lord" (Rom 8:31–32, 35, 38–39).

I don't know many things; but I know what the promise is: "I have set my bow in the clouds, and it shall be a sign of the covenant between me and the earth" (Gen 9:13). *Why should I be discouraged?*

Bibliography

Alexander, Michelle. *The New Jim Crow: Mass Incarceration in the Age of Colorblindness*. New York: New Press, 2012.

Branch, Taylor. *Parting the Waters: America in the King Years, 1954–63*. New York: Simon and Schuster, 1988.

Feuerbach, Ludwig. *The Essence of Christianity*. Translated by George Eliot. New York: Dover, 2008.

Meeks, M. Douglas. *God the Economist: The Doctrine of God and Political Economy*. Minneapolis: Fortress, 1989.

———. *Origins of the Theology of Hope*. Minneapolis: Fortress, 1974.

Moltmann, Jürgen. *God in Creation: A New Theology of Creation and the Spirit of God*. Translated by Margaret Kohl. Minneapolis: Fortress, 1993.

32. Ibid., 149.

―――. *The Trinity and the Kingdom:The Doctrine of God*. Translated by Margaret Kohl. Minneapolis: Fortress, 1993.

―――. *The Way of Jesus Christ: Christology in Messianic Dimensions*. Translated by Margaret Kohl. Minneapolis: Fortress, 1993.

Wright, N. T. *The New Testament and the People of God*. Minneapolis: Fortress, 1992.

Young, Crawford. *The African Colonial State in Comparative Perspective*. New Haven: Yale University Press, 1997.

11

Economy, Violence, and Culture of Peace

NÉSTOR O. MÍGUEZ

The Actuality of the Topic

If you do the following Internet search: culture + economics + violence, you will find more than 15 million entries in Spanish and more than 112 million in English. Over a million of these entries are academic articles. Many books have been published on various facets of the issue, so much so that it is almost impossible to compose a comprehensive bibliography on the subject. However, if one adds the word *theology* to the same search, one will see the number reduced to just 10 percent of the original, and further reduced to just 1 percent when one specifies Christian theology. A cursory reading will show that the majority of these studies are case studies, linked to ethnic, sexual, or other forms of visible violence. The search field will narrow further when you add words like *globalization*, *market*, or other such indicators of the economic system. These articles that point to the universal dimension of this issue, however, are themselves marginalized, falling outside mainstream contemporary theology, appearing only as they relate to the ecological concern in so-called "liberation theologies," especially those called "postcolonial."

In the minds of many, the majority of Christians, and even theologians who reflect on profound themes of faith, these are isolated topics, only tangentially related. Douglas Meeks is one of the few who have shown that such an oversight results in the loss of fundamental aspects of our theological understanding, even in such topics as our understanding of

Trinitarian doctrine.[1] As Giorgio Agamben has demonstrated, this same Western economic and political worldview has been informed by theological discussions within Christianity.[2] The necessary "temporal autonomy" goes against its own origins in Christian thought, especially as developed from the sixteenth-century Protestant Reformation on. Today, a politically and economically informed ethic requires that we recognize both the relative autonomy as well as the inevitable tension between theology, politics, and the economy.

As a crucial nuance, I would like to stress that we cannot venture into these issues without considering in what ways violence has been transformed into a weapon in service of the economic domain in the construction of the empire of late capitalism, which is imposed today, not without resistance, as a universal *patron*—meaning both an owner with power and a pattern to follow. This is not new. The Greek historian Polybius called Rome an empire for its "desire for dominion in order to plunder." Economy and violence—viewed both theoretically and from our "Third World" experience as those who have lived with repression in Latin America and have sought alternatives—are very closely linked topics. Violence does not appear as a "natural" phenomenon anywhere, if there is not an economic, political, and cultural context that controls, supports, or incites it. Human violence is always cultural, never "natural." Human actions are mediated by symbolic schemes for discursive dimensions that give meaning, justification, and presence and are then projected as historical data. Nature is not "violent" in terms of value; only the human being distinguishes "violent" acts from those that are not. Religion is not exempt from this symptom: there is a symbolic violence in which religion plays a prominent role, even if not foundational.[3]

Culture and Violence

Given the brevity of this essay, I would like to sketch a few points that will orient us in our treatment of the violence-culture relationship. Broadly defined, violence is any action, physical or symbolic, exercised in use of some power or force over a person, sector, group, or social institution, which forces the will of the other and puts at risk the integrity and life of another.

1. Meeks, *God the Economist*.
2. Agamben, *The Kingdom and the Glory*.
3. Girard, *Violence and the Sacred*.

Of course, the literature on the relationship of violence to culture is almost endless, drawing from anthropology, psychoanalysis, social history, sociology, political science, and so forth. I will limit myself simply to highlighting a few significant aspects of our topic, starting with the assertion that culture "contains" violence:

- Culture "contains" violence when it establishes forms, rules, and institutions to limit or sublimate it.

- Culture "contains" violence insofar as all cultures include tolerated and even encouraged forms of violence.

- Therefore thinking about a "culture of peace" means seeking cultural forms that can act to contain violence in the first sense and to reduce the violent content in the second sense.

With this starting point, we propose other premises regarding the topic:

- Culture and economics are not independent fields. The idea that some economists posit that the economy is "natural," that it has its own value-less laws, free from the intervention of ethical issues, is totally false. A clear example is private land ownership and the way in which in the West, from Aristotle, St. Thomas, or John Locke, property has been linked with freedom. Laws express culturally and ethically established relationships, like power relations between different sectors of society. Economic practices (among others) in a society lay down a "matrix" of socially permissible conduct that goes beyond mere law. They establish *habitus* and ways of relating to each other (clientele practices, formulas for manners). Corruption is also a "cultural-economic" space where violence is particularly evident.

- The economy, for its particular role in the subsistence and reproduction of human life (physical, cultural, and social life), bears an extraordinary responsibility in the modes of violence.

- The law justly distinguishes between "natural death" and "violent death," the second being actionable. However, the distinction is also culturally established: starvation in the desert is "natural," but it is "violence" if a child dies of starvation in the city. In this second case, food is available but behavioral barriers (physical, symbolic, legal) are imposed between the person and the food. If a mother dies in childbirth it is "natural," and the child is not accused of murder. Yet if there are hospital resources to avoid it and it is not, then it is an actionable and "violent" act. The law, as the Apostle Paul very well discovered, may in itself be violent or enable violence when, in its exercise, it lowers the quality of life or risks the lives of others. Like culture, we can say that the law at times "contains violence."

- The economy also includes forms of violence. From the moment it is charged with the production, distribution, and provision for consumption of goods necessary for life, if that production and distribution or if the forms of consumption threaten the lives of some human beings, it can be said to be a "regulator" of (in technical terms: it admits or controls) violence.

Thus, we can distinguish three ways in which the relationship between economics and violence is established.

First, violence intrinsic to the economic system. If violence is behaving in a way that endangers the lives of others, then any form of economy based on the accumulation of resources by one sector and denial of them to others contains in itself a degree of violence. Consider the scenario in which one group of people is "poor" as a whole, and all experience similar shortages. Even when they all suffer, no one has taken away the goods necessary for the life of others. This fact prevents us from calling this violence. Yet if the goods necessary to ensure the life of the group exist, and some deny them to others (whatever be the manner and justifications), this reveals a substrate of violence, which can manifest itself as physical violence or can be regulated as symbolic violence.

In today's globalized world, there are no more "closed economies." Instead, the world is viewed as a single interconnected economic field and the possibility of a total global market is even encouraged. Given this, it should be noted that the measure of inequitable distribution (which is inherent in the current financial capitalist system) generates violence intrinsic to the system on the global scale. As Juan Torres López, a Spanish economist from the group Economistas por la Paz y la Seguridad,[4] writes,

> The United States imposes itself as an indispensable nation, as the nucleus from which must stem decisions and economic rules that others must obey. Just 5 percent of the world population consumes nearly 50 percent of the global supply of gasoline and also appropriates half of the wealth produced in the world. It thereby creates an imperial power that not everyone in the rest of the world is willing to accept when it means injustice, suffering, misery and growing inequality. The result is the asymmetric world in which

4. See http://www.eumed.net/paz/index.htm.

we live, where the richest 1 percent enjoys 57 percent of the income while the poorest 80 percent only gets 16 percent of the
wealth. These are the conditions in which, like it or not, a general
climate of violence is emerging. The dominant response, however,
is pressing the accelerator of reforms that strengthen the market,
reduce social spending, reduce the protection of the marginalized
and promote work that degrades and leads directly to poverty and
the exclusion of hundreds of millions of families worldwide. That
is to say, a genuine war economy to the extent that it creates a
violence of necessity.[5]

The statistical facts presented by the United Nations report on economics and poverty are equally dramatic. From this report it follows that
the problem of violence is not only a problem of poverty or social marginalization (the violence is carried out by the poor) but rather fundamentally
a problem generated by income distribution. So while Africa is the poorest
continent, it is not the most violent in terms of street violence, criminality,
or domestic violence (political or racial violence is something else, with
other concurrent motives). Latin America, which has higher "per capita"
income compared to Asia and Africa, has, in these same categories, a higher
crime index. Yet it is also the continent with the greatest polarization between the rich and the poor, the most unequal distribution of income. The
hypothesis supported by most scholars of Latin American crime is that the
increase in criminal violence comes from the projection in society of this
unfair distribution of wealth, where privation coexists with squandering.
To this we must add the issue of the proliferation of drug trafficking that
also has an essentially economic component. This intrinsic configuration of
current global capitalism forms the basis for what I propose as the second
way economics and violence are related.

Second, violence that appears extrinsic to the economic system but
linked to it all the same. As this is a topic of heated debate, even in current
social studies on criminality, I refer extensively to a study done in Chile;
however, it can be applied, with minor variations, to all of Latin America.

The impact of the global economic crisis has undeniable repercus-
sions on the way common crime is expressed, particularly in ecological-
economic areas more directly linked to the world capitalist economy.
Similarly, the type of economy, in our case the neoliberal economy, limits
the beneficent action of the State toward those in poverty and extreme

5. López, "Economía de guerra, economía de la paz."

poverty, increasingly discarding the possibility of implementing a more permeable structure of opportunities. Effectively and in quantitative terms, it was possible to demonstrate statistically that in Chile, between 1974 and 1990, the prison population tripled. I suggest an association between this and the global economic crisis of 1980–82 and the implementation of a staunch neoliberal economic system, beginning in the eighties.

We should highlight some aspects of a new criminological theoretical proposal that we have developed, one that complements our theory of the subcultural continuum of crime, relative to common delinquency of the underworld. That is, the counterculture of the lower-class thieves constitutes a particular expression of the illegal countercultural economic alternative to normative economics. In this illegal countercultural economic alternative of delinquents, the proletariat underclass and the marginal and marginalized find alternative work roles that allow for this counterculture, which is based on an alternative illegal economic system. This is currently the case not only in Chile but throughout Latin America and in all countries where the normative neoliberal economic system is unable to incorporate the proletariat underclass and the marginalized.

In the context of a comparative analysis of male convicts in the Metropolitan Region (Gran Santiago), we can see that the tally of the economic damage done by the middle-class inmates (40 cases) who have committed crimes against property reached the sum of 41,365,428,797 CLP (Chilean pesos), which means an economic harm of 1,034,135,719 CLP per person. Meanwhile, the lower-class inmates (1,959 cases) totaled 1,285,569,968 CLP in economic damage, which translates into a total of 730,437 CLP per single offender, according to estimations in 1997 dollars. That is, each middle-class inmate caused 1,415 times more economic harm than a lower-class inmate.

In our view, however, it is the common crimes that blatantly reveal (being an empirical measure) the global economic system crisis and the increase of poverty and social marginalization. This is in the context of the staunch imposition of the neoliberal economic system, including an increasingly less and less relevant role for a reduced State as benefactor. The common crimes against property are those that increase, given the growing marginalization and extreme poverty of the proletariat underclass. From our point of view, these deviations have to do with the marginal youth gangs' learned despair and forms of delinquency, which are expressions of an informal and illegal economy that facilitates survival in the subcultural world of a poverty without alternatives.

I do not deny other effects of the violence generated by drug trafficking, which feeds on unemployment and youth on the streets. It is bolstered further by situations of domestic violence, the poor fighting against the poor, and sports violence. These are just some of the many problems one could mention that, at least to a large degree, find their origin in the economic conditions generated by the system. We do not have enough space here to do more than mention them. The phenomenon of drug trafficking is incredibly important, especially in the last twenty years, as it coincides with the wider implementation of the neoliberal system in Latin America (policies that today are being revisited by several so-called populist governments: Chavez, Lula, Morales, Fernández de Kirchner, Correa). This growing violence, established in Latin America (the area I know, but the observation by extension holds elsewhere) and generated by the trade of addictive substances, has marked not only the issue of crime and violence but has influenced all areas of culture. Without going into a detailed analysis of the subject (which is not my specialty), we can point to several factors:

- Since this is an illegal market, it generates a very large space of illegality, as wide as its economic importance. Therefore, it is necessarily linked to crime and violent crime. This marginality obviously will impact the marginal spaces, creating an economic network that lives and grows on the margins of the State and accordingly needs to generate institutions (cartels, mafias) that regulate it.

- This being a market with a lot of money (one of the largest worldwide trades in terms of the amount of foreign currency being moved), this trade affects the fluidity of others. In fact, the money laundering mechanisms (which take the form of commercial transactions in so-called tax havens as much as investments in areas such as sports and art) prove to be competition to "legal" economies.

- The social effects, especially among the poorest sectors of the population, are devastating. The destruction of solidarity networks among the poor is generated by the presence of an illegal sector that uses poverty and the poor as its shield. The increase in armed violence, the proliferation of weapons of war in the poorest neighborhoods, infighting among cartels and their "settling of accounts," and its extension to people not directly involved, have changed the meaning and mode of social work, political affiliation, and citizenship structure in these enclaves. In turn, we see elevated levels of insecurity that feed repressive governments, the establishment of police states, and the so-called war on the poor.

- At the political level, it has produced a reversal of the economic logic under the power games in which it occurs. That is, while economic theory insists that once a market economy takes on an autonomous function, in which consumers and producers are supposedly mutually dependent, this logic falls apart with the drug market. The producers, who come primarily from "Third World" countries (e.g., Bolivia, Colombia), are pursued, and the consumers are not controlled since that would require strong intervention in the population of the affluent world where the majority of consumption exists. The control over production justifies political, economic, and even military interventions by rich and imperial countries, especially by the United States, in the poorest countries. To proceed in the opposite way—that is, attacking the consumption in order to break up drug trafficking—would lead to questions that would unite economy and culture: What leads an affluent and educated population (note the massive drug abuse among college students, celebrities, and others) to consume narcotics to such a great extent? What psycho-cultural, anthropological, and social factors, what personality structures are generated in advanced capitalist countries that engender such a high rate of consumption that narcotics trafficking constitutes one of the largest sectors of the transnational global market? Surely the factors that trigger this population's consumption differ from those that induce drug production or use in marginal populations of the poor. Yet it is easier to persecute indigenous coca growers in Bolivia or Colombia than to take on these questions and to seek coherent answers. Thus, the solutions proposed involve violence on the poor for problems that come from the market and the culture of the rich.

The drug market is an exaggerated and paradoxical expression of what actually is the economic concept that sustains the globalized world. For the neoliberal system, the logic of the whole market, this is necessary if we are to assume the true final realization (almost raised in evolutionary terms) of the human species; that is, it is necessary to affirm its profoundly individualist rationality. This expresses its "natural" condition. Economic theories that seek to sustain the neoliberal system have, among other ideological assumptions, the idea that the economy responds to certain laws that are in some way imprinted in human nature. The real human being, in Hobbesian style, only exists in profound competition with other human beings. This competition—omnipresent and all-embracing—is what organizes society. Selfishness allows life, and she who seeks to interfere and regulate it ends up instead destroying it. Sin has been elevated to the place of virtue, and love of neighbor is an impossible hindrance that would only lead to ruin and distress. The human being is, philosophically speaking, a being to/for "itself." But contrary to what "being for itself" is in Marxism or in existentialism, in neoliberalism it can be said that this being "for itself" has nothing to do with its consciousness of being but rather with its inexhaustible selfishness, an unlimited ambition for possession. The person "is" to the extent to which she possesses. To be free is to be an owner. Only free competition in all spheres of life produces true freedom. This is a "gift" of the free market, though there is nothing free in the free market. Any interference only ends up altering the potential expression of the person. It is not difficult to see the theological implications of these assumptions.

When we try to organize things from other starting points and we impose foreign rules on this game of interests, says F. von Hayek, the greatest theoretician in this area, it only complicates matters. The result is confusion, oppression, and misery. The "invisible hand of the market" must be made safe from any interference. Thus the State (and therefore politics) should be reduced to its minimum expression. It is the same for unions, because they restrict freedom of negotiations between the employer and the worker by including corporate interests foreign to the market itself (as if the labor market survived only on individual contracts). Other institutions should exist at the bare minimum necessary to allow for the market to operate freely. The State functions like a police force that guarantees the property of those who own it (without inquiring how they came to be property owners), and that is where the government's meddling must end. "Less state, more freedom" is the anarchist cry of the powerful.

Of course, this represents the interests of the wealthy classes, those who hoard more than 85 percent of the goods and services worldwide, even though they constitute less than 15 percent of the population. These global elites impose their desires and consumption patterns on the rest. Thus, the remaining 85 percent are driven to think that the good life is consuming what the rich consume; and they end up captive to that desire. It is the new form of slavery. In ancient times slaves were chained with iron shackles.

In industrial capitalism, workers were held captive by the chains of wages that subjected them to exploitation by their bosses. In today's consumerist capitalism, the instrument of subjugation is within the person. It is the captivity of desire. The person is influenced, through propaganda and social pressure of the dominant ideologies, to behave like a compulsive consumer. The consumer of goods is never satisfied, because the logic of established anxiety requires that just when one buys a product, another product appears encouraging a new desire. Thus an ethos of anguish is established that is the flipside of violence. On the other hand, we see violence against the ecosystem as well because this matrix of consumption poisons the planet with waste.

Democracy is the free market, said the Bush administration, and thus imposed such "liberty" with blood and fire in many countries (and although less explicit, it remains the policy of the Obama administration as well). This is done by the most powerful and indebted government in the world, with an exorbitant military system that serves as a universal police officer. This combination of military, economic, and political strength allied with neoliberal business interests is what we call "Empire." In the name of postmodern "liberty," this Empire invades countries, commits genocides, and calls it "collateral damage," while also combating "terrorism" with acts of terror. What neoliberalism supports is one thing, but what its beneficiaries do with it is another thing altogether. They are the heirs of the hypocrisy of the Pharisees. The god of the Market does not survive without human sacrifices: the subjection of the living to its policies that result in hunger and millions dead among the poor and disinherited of the world.

This gospel according to Hayek, with its parallels in Milton Friedman and other neoliberal ideologues, is the anti-Gospel. "Blessed are the rich, happy are the powerful, for the kingdom of this earth is theirs." For them, selfishness is a saving virtue and love is a mortal sin. The Other is a threat to my liberty. The only human concern should be to realize one's own desires (even though it is actually a desire induced by propaganda, the true "will of the flesh," the Apostle Paul would say). The tension between the various interests in dispute is resolved only through free competition, they say. The invisible hand of the market will take care of all things. Yet this brings in the long and the short term, the triumph of one and the annihilation of the other. What the neoliberal proposal does not explain is that when the competition is for vital goods, losing means frustration, helplessness, and death.

That is, the economic system generates a violence "external" to itself starting from the dramatic internal violence that condemns an increasingly large sector of the population to exclusion. This exclusion means being denied access to the goods necessary to sustain life plus the "show effect" that occurs upon seeing others with an overabundance of these same necessary goods. Violence is established as the system's logic when the delinquent realizes: if my life is not worthy (and thus, they deprive me of what is necessary to support it), why would the life of others be worthy? This is a sinister logic taught by the system.

Third, there is an economic construct of violence. Violence itself has been established as a prominent economic factor. This has been the case since the seizure of "the spoils of war" and the capture of slaves and so on. Yet the intensity has increased in capitalism due to the "industrial war complex." In this discussion it is not a small matter that the weapons business controls the financial system around the world. War is a disaster for the people but a business for speculators in the arms field. If just a quarter of what the "allied nations" invested in military spending in Iraq would have been spent on food, health, education, and infrastructure, the quality of life for Iraqis would have been greatly improved. As it later became clear, the war was not launched for the alleged strategic reasons and much less for the supposed humanitarian and democratic reasons. Rather, it was stimulated by arms dealers and the petroleum market and also by a culture of violence that is easy to observe in the United States. The violence was essential to keeping the Western energy system running in the quantities to which transnational industries and Western lifestyles have grown accustomed. In addition to this, violence is established in the logic of the imperial mind that spills over in everyday violent acts.

I remember being in Washington, DC, as a visiting professor in 1999 when the Columbine school shooting occurred. I saw President Clinton's press conference on television, in which, with conviction, he said, "We must teach our young people that they cannot solve problems with violence, killing people." In the same news broadcast, a few minutes later, the same president justified the bombings by the United States Air Force in the former Yugoslavia. The next day, I asked my students how many had seen the same news report. When asked what peculiarity they had noticed, no one could identify the contradiction between the two statements. The political and economic violence was completely naturalized; they could not see the profound connection that a culture of violence established between this violence and the violence of everyday life.

Even when other means were available, violence, the show of unyielding force and the right of the powerful to dispose of the lives of others, is characteristic of the culture and mentality of Empire, which governs both the military logic and economic logic. This is why war and other forms of violence are a "business" and an inseparable part of the current economic system. Because of the effects of globalization, violence as an economy that is imposed affects all human relationships. As Juan Torres López writes,

> The present war has the same networking characteristics as almost all contemporary phenomena. War is also globalized and its damages and effects of all kinds extend in a greater measure, in an intersecting manner and without confinement to localized areas and social dimensions. . . . I believe war is becoming a phenomenon that is more dissipated, no longer a specific moment of conflict but rather a permanent state of violence. Such violence is business for some, even as it is death for many.[6]

Toward a Culture of Peace

From our biblical perspective, the possibility of human life depends on a culture of peace as opposed to this present culture and economy of violence. Certainly it is not possible to speak of a "biblical position" without qualification, since in the Bible there are different perspectives and approaches to this issue. Because human history has been interwoven with violence, no one can speak of any human experience, or even the experience of God, that is not marked by elements of violence.

I'm not interested in entering a debate about whether violence is constitutive of human life, woven through by way of original sin and the original murder in the story of Abel and Cain, or if a social life without violence is even possible. I start from the fact that today we are living in the midst of great violence. If such levels of violence are not moderated and if a new cultural space capable of channeling violence doesn't emerge, all human life is at risk. Violence will end up being violence that devours its own author, as Paul warned in Gal 5:13–15: "For you were called to freedom, brothers and sisters; only do not use your freedom as an opportunity for self-indulgence, but through love become slaves to one another. For the

6. López, "Economía de guerra, economía de la paz."

whole law is summed up in a single commandment, 'You shall love your neighbor as yourself.' If, however, you bite and devour one another, take care that you are not consumed by one another." Expanding our definition beyond the human realm, we cannot ignore that violence toward all creation and toward human beings as an inseparable part of that creation is part of this threat (Rom 8:19–23).

Understanding "Peace"

"Peace" in the Bible is both a means and a goal of cultural construction. *Peace* (Hebrew *shalom*; Greek *eirene*) is a packed word in the biblical tradition. On one hand, it was the daily greeting of friends who met each other, the simple recognition of the other: it is our Spanish "hola," our English "hi" or our Italian "ciao." Yet it is also the desire for good, the expression of sympathy with which one receives a guest or announces a visit. Thus we find it in a very special way in the greeting the Risen Christ gave the frightened disciples (John 20:19).

Yet the extent of the meaning of "peace" does not end there. The sleep of death is also seen as *shalom* (Gen 15:15). In its deepest meaning, however, God's shalom is not of death but of life. It is the announcement and hope of the joy of the best of life. The images that decorate the word *peace* in the texts of the Hebrew Scriptures go beyond the state of quietness and calmness understood by the Western tradition. Its semantic path, the plurality of meanings that it holds, includes the idea of wholeness, wellness, and prosperity. Psalm 128 summarizes peace in the description of a blessed life (although we recognize the patriarchal tone typical of that time): "Blessed is everyone who fears the LORD, who walks in his ways. You shall eat the fruit of the labor of your hands; you shall be happy, and it shall go well with you. Your wife will be like a fruitful vine within your house; your children will be like olive shoots around your table. Thus shall the man be blessed who fears the LORD. The LORD bless you from Zion. May you see the prosperity of Jerusalem all the days of your life. May you see your children's children. Peace be upon Israel!"

For this very reason, there will never be peace as long as injustice endures. There is no peace without justice. Peace and justice call for each other. "Steadfast love and faithfulness will meet; righteousness and peace will kiss each other" (Ps 85:10). Peace and justice are the gifts of God in response to the faithfulness of God's people, and they are announced as the ultimate expression of the will of God. "May the mountains yield prosperity for the people, and the hills, in righteousness" (Ps 72:3). Peace is part of the messianic promise: "His authority shall grow continually, and there shall be endless peace for the throne of David and his kingdom. He will establish and uphold it with justice and with righteousness from this time onward and forevermore. The zeal of the Lord of hosts will do this" (Isa 9:7).

Both the Psalms and the prophets observe the infidelity of the people, especially the breaking of God's will by the powerful, who twist and violate judgment and justice. So we will see those who announce a false peace to hide their crimes: "Do not drag me away with the wicked, with those who are workers of evil, who speak peace with their neighbors, while mischief is in their hearts" (Ps 28:3). Jeremiah says the same thing, announcing the imminent destruction of Jerusalem: "They have treated the wound of my people carelessly, saying, 'Peace, peace,' when there is no peace" (Jer 6:14). This is why we can say that there is no peace without blessing in the tradition of Israel. There is no peace when power commits abuses or when the weak are deprived. Again and again prophets and poets remind us that the shalom that God intends is not quietness, not stillness and repose, but rather requires dynamism, work committed to the divine purpose in creation, a force that sustains life.

Western languages have not given the same power to the word *peace*. The plurality of the Hebrew meanings does not allow for a single translation. Proof of this is that while the translators of the Septuagint often used *eirene* for shalom, they also sought other words to translate it depending on the context: *soteria* ("salvation," Gen 26:31 and others, especially regarding offerings); *hileos* ("mercy," Gen 43:23 and others); *hygiaino* ("be healthy," Exod 4:18; 1 Sam 25:6).

Outside of the biblical context, the Greek *eirene* indicates a time without conflict, the absence of war, an agreement between two peoples, camps, or villages that enables a stable relationship without aggression. In another sense, it becomes more of a virtue of a certain peace and stillness that allows one to live without anxiety (*ataraxia*). That is why, in ancient pre-Christian Greek texts, we find the word *eirene* to be accompanied by other words to complete the concept: "peace and prosperity," "peace and security," "peace and honor."

In the time of Jesus, the word *peace* was part of the political propaganda of the Roman Empire. The *Pax Augusta* justified imperial dominion. The imperial motto stated that this *Pax Romana* was the (imposed) gift that Rome offered to other peoples. That peace was identified with the *pax deorum*, the agreement of the gods to bless, with the praise of victory, the Roman armies.

This Roman ideal of peace, which has been adopted by subsequent empires even to this very day, is reflected in the maxim *vis pacem, para bellum* (if you want peace, prepare for war). This is how the powerful and the conquerors justify their war machines. It is the slogan that announces the abstruse character of preemptive wars. According to an apologist for this same Roman Empire, Tacitus, an expression of this destructive peace can be heard in the words of the defeated Briton chief Calgacus, who said of the Romans, "where they make a desert, they call it peace."[7] Some have compared this with the now widespread *Pax Americana*. However, in the mindset of today's Empire, violence that pacifies is related to business: "they make a business, and call it peace."

The peace Jesus offers is contrasted with the peace of world, the peace imposed by the "prince of this world" (John 14:27–31). The peace that the world or the Empire offers is founded on violence, and therefore it is not authentic peace. This violence culminates in brutality, dealing death to the very body of Jesus. By contrast, the peace Jesus offers is not based on an expression of superiority, a capacity for imposition, an ability in wielding weapons, or the development of military technology. The peace Jesus offers is framed as an abundance of life for all, as loving equity, as shared freedom. It is not only an individual virtue or the exclusive rights of one race, creed, or class but rather a way to understand the meaning and goal of human life. The peace granted to those who trust in the way of Jesus allows the fear of a peace imposed by arms to be overcome. It is a peace that finds joy in unity with God the Father, in love toward brothers and sisters as a commandment. It is the way Jesus himself builds peace: He does what the Father has commanded.

The greeting by which the resurrected Christ reveals himself to his own (John 20:19–23) is precisely that of shalom, an announcement of peace that is completed in three acts: the certainty of life as a gift of God to be preached to all nations ("I send you"), the presence of a Spirit that revives the creation ("Receive the Holy Spirit"), and the possibility of a forgiveness that renews human relationships ("the sins you forgive, they shall be forgiven").

7. Tacitus, *Life of Agricola*, 29–32.

In interpreting the meaning of the messiahship of Jesus, Paul brings forth new ramifications, seeing that the Reign of Christ multiplies itself in fruits of peace. This thought reaches its greatest depth in the letters to the Colossians and to the Ephesians, which is reflected in the statement that affirms, "For he is our peace . . . , thus making peace and [reconciling] both groups to God in one body through the cross, thus putting to death that hostility through it. So he came and proclaimed peace to you who were far off and peace to those who were near" (Eph 2:14–17). A "culture of peace" is not an abstraction, a spiritual aura, or a religious subjectivity. It has to be embedded, as in every culture, in the political and economic spheres. In the biblical text itself the prophet Isaiah highlights these dimensions.

A culture of peace is not possible without establishing a fairer distribution system. As we read in Isa 32:17, "The effect of righteousness will be peace, and the result of righteousness, quietness and trust forever." Several other biblical passages in the prophets, the Psalms, the Gospels, and the letters of Paul follow this line of thought. In the New Testament, a culture of peace is linked to the idea of the "Reign of God," which is a relational form where the other is both the subject and object of love and the setting for justice. Violence, as we have defined it as the risk and destruction of another's life, is the opposite of God's reign. Thus, Isaiah says, "How the faithful city has become a whore! She that was full of justice, righteousness lodged in her—but now murderers! Your silver has become dross, your wine is mixed with water. Your princes are rebels and companions of thieves. Everyone loves a bribe and runs after gifts. They do not defend the orphan, and the widow's cause does not come before them" (Isa 1:21–23). In contrast, justice is understood in the Bible as the establishment of relationships of symmetry and reciprocity that ensure everyone's life. Peace appears as its fruit: fullness of life. Isaiah 1:15–19 shows this dimension to be the true worship of God:

> When you stretch out your hands,
> I will hide my eyes from you;
> even though you make many prayers,
> I will not listen;
> your hands are full of blood.
> Wash yourselves; make yourselves clean;
> remove the evil of your doings
> from before my eyes;

cease to do evil;
    learn to do good;
seek justice,
    rescue the oppressed,
defend the orphan,
    plead for the widow.

Come now, let us argue it out,
    says the LORD:
though your sins are like scarlet,
    they shall be like snow;
though they are red like crimson,
    they shall become like wool.
If you are willing and obedient,
    you shall eat the good of the land.

The "widow and orphan" appear here as the clearest examples of the weak and threatened. Other texts include references to the poor, the stranger, and to other forms of oppression. The justice of an economic system, in prophetic revelation, is always measured by the situation of the weakest. These are the "excluded" in the biblical vocabulary. A culture of peace will be centered in the situation of the least protected, where life appears most severely threatened, because violence is precisely the threat to life. Thus, Isaiah delivers a text that Jesus of Nazareth later makes his own: "The spirit of the Lord God is upon me, because the Lord has anointed me; he has sent me to bring good news to the oppressed, to bind up the brokenhearted, to proclaim liberty to the captives, and release to the prisoners; to proclaim the year of the Lord's favor" (Isa 61:1–2).

As we have noted, violence, even more than poverty, feeds on inequity. The accumulation system we experience today, unprecedented in world history, is in itself the index for and source of the degree of violence that this system generates. Again Isaiah warns, "Ah, you who join house to house, who add field to field, until there is room for no one but you, and you are left to live alone in the midst of the land!" (Isa 5:8). This warning concerning the absurdity of excessive accumulation of goods is valid even though this same inequality in the distribution of political power makes this violence "legal": "Ah, you who make iniquitous decrees, who write oppressive statutes, to turn aside the needy from justice and to rob the poor of my people of their right, that widows may be your spoil, and that you may make the orphans your prey!" (Isa 10:1–2). On the opposite side, honoring the life that God has created is true worship to the God who created the world and life:

> Is not this the fast that I choose:
> > to loose the bonds of injustice,
> > to undo the thongs of the yoke,
> to let the oppressed go free,
> > and to break every yoke?
> Is it not to share your bread with the hungry,
> > and bring the homeless poor into your house;
> when you see the naked, to cover them,
> > and not to hide yourself from your own kin?
> Then your light shall break forth like the dawn,
> > and your healing shall spring up quickly;
> your vindicator shall go before you,
> > the glory of the LORD shall be your rear guard.
> Then you shall call, and the LORD will answer;
> > you shall cry for help, and he will say, Here I am.
>
> If you remove the yoke from among you,
> > the pointing of the finger, the speaking of evil,
> if you offer your food to the hungry
> > and satisfy the needs of the afflicted,
> then your light shall rise in the darkness
> > and your gloom be like the noonday. (Isa 58:6–10)

Denaturalizing Selfishness and Violence: A Culture of Peace

A culture of peace should include several facets, but here we will concentrate on the economic realm. Creating a culture of peace must include establishing mechanisms that supplement the economy, limiting the power of the market in order to ensure a gradaul increase in economic equity. The "total market" mechanism, contrary to what the theorists say, has resulted in the absolute growth of accumulation and exclusion. It is necessary to put limits on the possibility for accumulation, on the appropriation by different economic sectors of resources that are necessary for the life of all. Privatizations lead to greater corruption, given that they are corrupting the very foundations of public ethics. Again, I cite Juan Torres López, who, toward the conclusion of his essay, writes,

> Fighting violence in any of its forms means building peace decently, not limiting yourself to destroying the enemy that you yourself have created. And peace necessarily requires a different type of economic relations based on equality and sharing in order to be able to eradicate misery and to be able to devote the necessary resources, even if it costs the privilege of the most wealthy, to meet the needs of all human beings without exception.[8]

In the faith of the Gospel, we do not think that we build the Reign of God. Yet we know that we have to live it as a real dimension in our personal lives. We have to project it in the social order as a testimony of our own respect for the image of God created in each human being. A culture of peace is the offer of a renewed life, an appeal to overcome violence through justice, to rest in love and not in hatred and confrontation, to respect that all property is provisional because the one Lord of all is the creator and has placed it in the service of all God's creatures. Redefining the economy is not "breaking the laws of nature" but rather following the law of God. It is to begin to realize the vision for which we yearn: "He shall judge between the nations, and shall arbitrate for many peoples; they shall beat their swords into plowshares, and their spears into pruning hooks; nation shall not lift up sword against nation, neither shall they learn war any more. O house of Jacob, come, let us walk in the light of the Lord!" (Isa 2:4–5).

Bibliography

Agamben, Giorgio. *The Kingdom and the Glory: For a Theological Genealogy of Economy and Government*. Stanford: Stanford University Press, 2011.

Girard, René. *Violence and the Sacred*. Translated by Patrick Gregory. Baltimore: Johns Hopkins University Press, 1979.

Hinkelammert, Franz. *Las armas ideológicas de la muerte*. Salamanca: Ediciones Sígueme, 1978.

Klein, Noami. *The Shock Doctrine: The Rise of Disaster Capitalism*. New York: Picador, 2008.

López, Juan Torres. "Economía de guerra, economía de la paz." http://www.eumed.net/paz/tepys/jtl.htm.

8. López, "Economía de guerra, economía de la paz."

Meeks, M. Douglas. *God the Economist: The Doctrine of God and Political Economy.* Minneapolis: Fortress, 1989.

Míguez Bonino, José. *Toward a Christian Political Ethics.* Philadelphia: Fortress, 1983.

Míguez, Néstor. *The Practice of Hope.* Translated by Aquíles Martínez. Minneapolis: Fortress, 2012.

Musti, Domenico. *Polibio e l'imperialismo romano.* Napoli: Ligouri Editori, 1978.

Torres López, Juan. "Economía de guerra, economía para la paz." *Temas para el Debate* 119 (October 2004). http://www.eumed.net/paz/tepys/jtl.htm.

12

A Culture of Life in the Dangers
of This Time[1]

JÜRGEN MOLTMANN

In this essay I grapple with what have been my most urgent concerns for
some time: a culture of life stronger than the terror of death, a love for life
that overcomes the destructive forces in our world today, and a confidence
in the future that overcomes doubt and fatalism. These issues are for me
most urgent because with the poet Friedrich Hölderlin I believe strongly:

> Wo aber Gefahr ist, wächst
> Das Rettende auch.
> [But where there is danger
> Salvation also grows.][2]

We should inquire whether and to what extent this hope bears weight as we
explore the possibilities of a culture of life in face of the real annihilations
with which our world is threatened. I will begin by addressing some of the
dangers of our time in Part I and in Part II offer some answers by considering dimensions of a world capable of supporting life and in a quite literal
sense a world that is worthy of love. At the end I return to the first verse of
the poem by Hölderlin: "Near is God, but difficult to grasp."[3]

---

1. Delivered as the Keynote Lecture at Beijing Forum 2010.
2. Hölderlin, "Patmos," lines 3–4.
3. Ibid., lines 1–2.

The Terror of Universal Death

The Unloved Life

Human life today is in danger. It is not in danger because it is mortal. Our life has always been mortal. It is in danger because it is no longer loved, affirmed, and accepted. The French author Albert Camus wrote after World War II, "This is the mystery of Europe: life is no longer loved."

I can attest to this. I remember the experiences of the war with continuing horror. My generation was destined for a murderous war in which it was no longer a matter of victory or peace but only of death. Those who suffered in that monstrous war knew what Camus meant: a life no longer loved is ready to kill and is liable to be killed. The survivors experienced the end of terror in 1945, but we had become so used to death that life took on a "take it or leave it" atmosphere because it had become meaningless.

The twentieth century was a century of mass exterminations and mass executions. The beginning of the twenty-first century saw the private terrors of senseless killings by suicide assassins. In the terrorists of the twenty-first century a new religion of death is confronting us. I do not mean the religion of Islam but rather the ideology of terror. "Your young people love life," said the Mullah Omar of the Taliban in Afghanistan, "our young people love death." After the mass murder in Madrid on March 11, 2004, there were acknowledgments by the terrorists with the same message: "You love life, we love death." A German who joined the Taliban in Afghanistan declared, "We don't want to win; we want to kill and be killed." Why? I think because they view killing as power and they experience themselves as God over life and death. This seems to be the modern terrorist ideology of the suicide assassins. It is also the mystery of crazed students who in the United States and Germany suddenly shoot their fellow students and teachers and end up taking their own lives.

I remember that we had this love of death in Europe some sixty years ago. "*Viva la muerte*," cried an old fascist general in the Spanish Civil War. Long live death! The German SS troops in the Second World War had the saying "Death gives, and death takes away" and wore the symbol of the skull and bones. It is not possible to deter suicide assassins, for they have broken the fear of death. They do not love life anymore, and they want to die with their victims.

Behind this terrorist ideological surface a greater danger is hidden: Peace, disarmament, and nonproliferation treaties between nations share an obvious assumption, namely, that on both sides there is the will to survive and the will to live. Yet what happens if one partner does not want to survive but is willing to die, if through death that partner can destroy this whole "wicked" or "godless" world? Until now we have had to deal only with an international network of suicide assassins and individual students overcome by a death wish. What happens when a nation possessing nuclear weapons becomes obsessed with this "religion of death" and turns into a collective suicide assassin against the rest of the human world because it is driven into a corner and gives up all hope? Deterrence works only so long as all partners have the will to live and want to survive. When it is of no matter whether one lives or dies, one has lost the fear that is necessary for deterrence. Whoever is convinced for religious reasons that he or she must become a sacrifice in order to save the world can no longer be threatened with death. The one who clamors for the "great war" even if it means one's own destruction is beyond deterrence.

The attraction of destroying a world that is considered "rotten," disordered, or godless can obviously grow into a universal death wish to which one sacrifices one's own life. "Death," then, becomes a fascinating divinity inflaming a desire for destruction. This apocalyptic "religion of death" is the real enemy of the will to live, the love of life, and the affirmation of being.

The Nuclear Suicide Program

Behind this present political danger endangering the common life of the nations there is still an older threat lurking: the nuclear threat. The first atomic bomb dropped on Hiroshima in August 1945 brought World War II to an end. At the same time, it marked the beginning of the end time for the whole of humankind. The end time is the age in which the end of humankind is possible at any moment. No human being could survive the "nuclear winter" that would follow a great atomic war. Remember that humankind was on the cusp of such a great atomic war for more than forty years during the Cold War. It is true that since the end of the Cold War in 1990 a great atomic war is not as likely. We live in relative peace. Yet there are still so many atomic and hydrogen bombs stored up in the arsenals of the great nations (and some smaller ones as well) that the self-annihilation of humankind remains a distinct possibility. Sakharov called it "collective suicide": "Whoever fires first, dies second." For those forty years we depended on "mutually assured destruction" for security.

Most people had forgotten this atomic threat until President Barack Obama, in a 2009 speech delivered in Prague, revived the old dream of a "world free of atomic bombs" and started new disarmament negotiations with Russia.[4] Then, many of us became aware again of this destiny hanging like a dark cloud over the nations. Strangely enough, we feel the presence of the nuclear threat publicly in what American psychologists call "nuclear numbing." We repress our anxiety, try to forget this threat, and live as if this danger were not there. Yet it is gnawing at our subconscious and impairing our love of life.

The Social Conditions of Misery

A general impairment of life also exists in miserable social conditions. For more than forty years we have heard repeatedly and everywhere the charge that, despite all political efforts, the "social gap between rich and poor" is widening. It is not just in the poorer countries of the Two-Thirds World that a small rich sector of the population rules over the masses of the poor. In the democracies of the developed world the financial asset gap between financiers, on the one hand, and low-income workers, welfare recipients, the unemployed, and those not able to work, on the other hand, takes on obscene proportions. Yet democracy is grounded not only in the freedom of citizens but also in their equality. Without social justice in life opportunities and the comparability of life circumstances the commonweal dies and with it what holds society together falls apart. Trust is lost.

Since the democratic revolutions in England, the United States, and France the political task in the European states has been the balancing of individual freedom and social equity. The deregulation of the economy and fiscal institutions wrought by American politics with all its destructive consequences has led to an imbalance between freedom and equality that has become life-threatening for many people. It has led to their disempowerment and poverty. A capitalism that is no longer politically controllable through the commonwealth becomes an enemy of democracy because it destroys the common meaning of the society. We find ourselves on a social slippery slope. Climbing on the social ladder brings anxiety. In the modern competitive society the losers fall off, the winners ascend, and "the winner takes all." The anxiety of life creates nothing but the anxiety of existence for

4. For the full text of Obama's speech, see http://www.huffingtonpost.com/2009/04/05/obama-prague-speech-on-nu_n_183219.html.

modern human beings. Yet is anxiety a good incentive for life, for work, and for happiness?

The Ecological Conditions of World Destruction

Unlike the nuclear threat, climate change is not only a threat but already an emerging reality everywhere. It is not only a latent problem but also very much a matter of public consciousness. People know it because they can see it, feel it, and sometimes smell it. The biosphere of the planet Earth is the only space we have for life. The globalization of human civilization has reached its limits and is beginning to alter the conditions of life on Earth.

The destruction of the environment that we are causing through our present global economic system will undoubtedly seriously jeopardize the survival of humanity in the twenty-first century. Modern industrial society has thrown out of balance the equilibrium of the earth's organism and is on the way to universal ecological death, unless we can change the way things are developing. Year after year vulnerable species of animals and plants die out. Scientists have shown that certain chemical emissions are destroying the ozone layer, while the use of chemical fertilizers and a multitude of pesticides is polluting our drinking water and making the soil infertile. They have shown that the global climate is already changing so that we now are experiencing an increasing number of "natural" catastrophes, such as droughts and floods, expanding deserts, and intense storms—catastrophes that are not simply natural but also caused by human activity. The ice in the Arctic and the Antarctic is melting. In the coming century scientists predict that coastal cities such as my hometown, Hamburg, and coastal regions such as Bangladesh and many South Seas islands will be flooded. All in all, life on this earth is under threat. Why is this so? With some irony one may say: Some do not know what they are doing, while others do not act on what they know.

This ecological crisis is fundamentally a crisis wrought by Western scientific and technological civilization. Yet it is a mistake to think that environmental problems are problems for the industrialized countries of the West alone. On the contrary, ecological catastrophes are intensifying even more in the midst of already existing economic and social problems of countries in the developing world. Indira Gandhi was right when she said, "Poverty is the worst pollution." Despite the well-documented "limits to growth," the ideology of permanent "growth" continues unabated with its specious promise of solving social problems. We know all this, but we are paralyzed and do not change our economy or our lifestyle. We do not do what we know is necessary to prevent the worst consequences. This paralysis may be called "ecological numbing." Nothing accelerates an imminent catastrophe so much as the paralysis of doing nothing.

We do not know whether humanity will survive this self-made destiny. This is actually a good thing. If we knew with certainty that we would not survive, we would do nothing; if we knew with certainty that we will survive, we would also do nothing. Only if the future is open for both possibilities are we forced to do today what is necessary to survive tomorrow. We cannot know whether humankind will survive, so we must act today as if the future of life depends on us and trust at the same time that our children and we will survive and thrive.

Must a human race exist or survive, or are we just an accident of nature? We can ask cynically: Didn't the dinosaurs come and go?

The Question of Existence:
Whether Humanity Should Be or Not Be?

More than seven billion human beings already live on Earth today. This number likely will grow rapidly. An alternative future is that the earth could be uninhabited. The earth existed without human beings for millions of years and may survive perhaps for millions of years after the human race disappears. This raises an even deeper question: Are we human beings on Earth only by chance, or are we human beings a "necessary" result of evolution? If nature would show a "strong anthropic principle," we could feel "at home in the universe" (Stuart Kauffman). If such a stark anthropological principle cannot be proved, the universe gives no answer to this existential question of humankind. Looking to the universe for an answer to the question of our reason for being, we encounter the sad conjecture of Steven Weinberg: "The more the Universe seems comprehensible, the more it also seems pointless." The silence of the world's expanses and the coldness of the universe can lead to our despondence. In any case neither the stars nor our genes say whether human beings should be or not be.

How can we love life and affirm our being as humans if humanity is only an accident of nature, superfluous and without relevance for the universe, perhaps only a mistake of nature? Is there a "duty to be," as Hans Jonas claimed? Is there any reason to love life and affirm the human being?

If we find no answer, every culture of life is uncertain in its fundamentals and built on shaky grounds.

A Culture of Life Must Be a Culture of Common Life in the Human and the Natural World

Can We "Live with the Bomb"?

Are the dangers growing faster than what can save us? I think we can grow in wisdom, but how? President Obama's dream of a "world without atomic weapons" is an honorable one, but only a dream. Human beings will never again become incapable of what they can do now. Whoever has learned the formula of atomic fission will never forget. Since Hiroshima in 1945, humankind has lost its "atomic innocence."

Yet the atomic end time is also the first common age of the nations. All the nations are sitting in the same boat. We all share the same threat. Everyone can become the victim. In this new situation, humankind must organize itself as the subject of common survival. The foundation of the United Nations in 1945 was a first step. International security partnerships can serve peace and give us time to live, and someday perhaps a transnational unification of humankind will keep the means of nuclear destruction under control. By science we learn to gain power over nature. By wisdom we learn to gain control of our power. The development of public and political wisdom is as important as scientific progress.

The first lesson we learn is this: Deterrence does not secure peace anymore. Only justice serves peace between the nations. There is no way to peace in the world except through just actions and harmonious balance of interests. Peace is not the absence of violence but the presence of justice. Peace is a process, not a property. Peace is a common way of reducing violence and constructing justice in the social and global relationships of humankind.

Social Justice Creates Social Peace

The gap between the poor and the rich widens, but the alternative to poverty is not property. The alternative to poverty and property is community. One can live in poverty when it is borne in common with others, as was the case in Europe in the years of hunger after the war. It is injustice that makes poverty insufferable. The spirit of communal solidarity and mutual help was demolished by flight from taxes, which in turn aroused the anger of the people. If everyone is in the same situation, then all give mutual help. Remove equality because one wins and the other loses, then mutual help also vanishes. By "community" here I mean the visible community of solidarity as well as the inner togetherness of society in social balance and social freedom. It is not football games that unite a society; it is social justice that creates lasting social peace.

The individualism that says "everyone is his or her own neighbor looking out for himself or herself" makes human beings powerless. The fragmenting of work by making it temporary, insecure, and without benefits harms the life planning of those at the mercy of the system and destroys their future. In communities of solidarity human beings are strong and wealthy, that is, wealthy in relationships with neighbors and friends, companions and colleagues on which one can depend. They are thus made strong by being recognized and by being esteemed as worthy. Many helpful actions emerge in such communities, such as child care, the care of the sick and aged, associations of the handicapped, and the hospice movement.

"Market position" and "competition" are certainly strong incentives for work, but they remain humane only in the framework of a common life, and that means only in the bounds of social and ecological justice. There are dimensions of life that may not be determined by the market logic because they follow other laws. Patients are not "customers" of doctors and nurses, and students are not "consumers" of the science and research of the university.

Reverence for Life

Because human society and the natural environment compose the total life system, when there is a crisis of dying in nature, a crisis of the whole life-system emerges as well. What we call today the "ecological crisis" is not only a crisis in our environment but also a total crisis of our life-system, and it cannot be solved by technological means only. It also demands a change in our lifestyle and a change in the basic values and convictions of our society. Modern industrial societies are no longer in harmony with the cycles and rhythms of the earth as was the case in premodern agrarian societies. Modern societies are predicated on progress and expansion of the projects of humanity. We reduce the nature of the earth to "our environment" and destroy the life-space of other forms of life. Nothing works so much destruction as reducing nature to no more than an environment for humans.

We need a change from the modern domination of nature to a "reverence for life," as Albert Schweitzer teaches us. "Reverence for life" is respect for every single form of life and for our common life in the human and the natural world and for the great community of all the living. A postmodern biocentrism will have to replace the Western and modern anthropocentrism. Of course, we cannot return to the cosmos-orientation of the ancient and premodern agrarian world, but we can begin the necessary ecological transformation of the industrial society. For this we must change our concept of time. The linear concept of progress in production, consumption, and waste must give way to the concept of the cyclical time of "renewable energy" and a "recycling economy." Only the cycles of life can give stability to our world of progress. Yet as long as the children of Ghana bear the burden of recycling our electronic scrap, we must say the recycling economy is still the economy of poor people. The 1992 Earth Charter of the United Nations points in the right direction: "Humanity is part of nature. All other life forms of nature have their worth independent of their worth for human beings." We are "part of nature" and can therefore only survive by preserving nature's integrity.

The Love of Life in Times of Danger

Human life is not only a gift of life but also a task of being human. To accept this task of humanity in times of terror requires the strength and courage to live. Life must be affirmed against terror and threat. To say it simply: Life must be lived and then the beloved life, which is the common life in the human and the natural world, will be stronger than the threat of universal annihilation. I see three major factors for this courage to be and the courage to live.

First, *human life must be affirmed, because it can also be denied.* As we know, a child can only grow and live in an atmosphere of affirmation. In an atmosphere of rejection, the child will fade away in soul and body. Experiencing affirmation is the occasion for a child to affirm himself or herself. What is true for the child is true for human beings throughout their lives. Where we are accepted, appreciated, and affirmed, we are motivated to live; where we feel a hostile world of contempt and rejection, we retire into ourselves and become defensive. We need a strong affirmation of life that can deal with such negations of life. Each *yes* to life is stronger than every negation of life, because it can create something new against the negations.

Second, *human life is participation.* We become alive where we feel the sympathy of others, and we stay alive where we share our life with others. As long as we are interested, we are alive. The counterproof is easy to make: indifference leads to apathy, and apathy is a sickness unto death. Complete lack of participation is a completely unlived life; it is the dying of the soul before physical death.

Third, *human life is alive in the pursuit of fulfillment.* Human life gains its dynamic from this inborn striving. "The pursuit of happiness" is, since the writing of the Declaration of Independence, one essential human right. To pursue one's happiness is not only a private human right but also a public human right as well. We speak of the "good life" or the "meaningful life," and we mean a life that lives out its best potential in the public life of a good and harmonious society. When we take this "pursuit of happiness" seriously, we encounter the misfortune of the masses of poor people and begin to suffer with the unfortunate. The compassion by which we are drawn into their passion for life is the reverse side of the pursuit of happiness. The more we become capable of the happiness of life, the more we become also capable of sorrow and compassion. This is the great dialectic of human life.

"But where there is danger, salvation also grows." How is salvation growing? I have tried to show how being can take in nonbeing, how life can overcome death through love, and how deadly contradictions can be changed into productive differences and higher forms of living and community. I am reminded of a famous statement of the German philosopher Friedrich Hegel, a friend of Hölderlin since their student time at Tübingen University. Hegel wrote in his *Phenomenology of the Mind* (1807),

> Not a life that shrinks away from death or remains untouched by
> devastations, but a life that endures death and bears death in itself
> is the life of the Spirit.

Consciously lived life is a beloved life that endures the contradictions of death and finds the courage to live through its dangers.

"Near Is God, and Difficult to Grasp"

Here at the end I will allow the theologian in me to speak with declarations of Christian faith:

- Should humanity be, or are we superfluous?

- Is there a duty to survive, or are life and death simply a "take it or leave it" matter?

- In the evolution of life are we an accident of life?

The existential questions of humankind are not only answered by rational arguments but first of all by prerational assurance or lack of assurance that leads the interests of our reason.

"Difficult to grasp is God," wrote Hölderlin, not because God is so distant from us human beings but, rather, "near" and therefore "difficult to grasp." What is "near," indeed nearer to us than we ourselves, is "not to be grasped" by us, for we would need distance for that. If we were, however, "grasped" by the nearness of God, we would know the answers to our existential questions:

- In the eternal *yes* of the living God we affirm our fragile and vulnerable humanity in spite of death.

- In the eternal love of God, we love life and resist its devastations.

- In the ungraspable nearness of God, we trust in what is saving even if dangers are growing.